JESUS CHRIST
Who Is, Who Was, and Who Is to Come!

VOL. 1

HELL AND HEAVEN
TESTIMONY BY SCIENTIST SARAH SEOH,

SARAH SEOH

ISBN: 978-1-4834-3141-3 (sc)

ISBN: 978-1-4834-3142-0 (e)

Library of Congress Control Number: 2015907541

Lulu Publishing Services rev. date: 5/28/2015

ABOUT THE AUTHOR

Sarah Seoh

(Name before becoming an ordained pastor: Sang-ah Seoh)

Sarah Seoh currently serves as a senior pastor at Lord's Love Christian Church in Los Angeles, California. Her relationship with God grows deeper every day. She evangelizes to others when she finds time. She plans to undertake a worldwide mission with her husband in the near future, if God allows.

1960 – Year of Birth

1980 – Graduated from Jin-Joo Girls' High School

1986 – Graduated from Ewha Women's University College of Medicine; obtained M.D. license

1989 – Received M.A. degree in Physiology from Seoul National University, College of Medicine

1993 – Received Ph.D. in Biology from the Medical School of Brown University

1993-1997 – Postdoctoral fellow in the School of Medicine at UCLA

2004 – Received M.Div. in Pastoral Theology in Talbot School of Theology

2004-Present – Head Pastor of Lord's Love Christian Church in Los Angeles, California

2009-Present – Director of L.A. New Person Spiritual Training Center

Recommendation Letter

"Let not your hearts be troubled. Believe in God; believe also in me. In my Father's house are many rooms. If it were not so, would I have told you that I go to prepare a place for you? And if I go and prepare a place for you, I will come again and will take you to myself, that where I am you may also be." (John 14:1-3)

Every Christian who believes in God and loves him has hope. The greatest hope among all would be the hope of Heaven. By no mistake it is the only hope for us, sojourners in this world, who have to go through a life that is full of suffering and worry. Today, there is a streak of light that brightens the hope within us.

The author, Sarah Seoh, received her education at prestigious schools and actively worked as a scientist until God called her to full-time ministry. While she was working for the Lord, she received special revelations from Him, which are written in this book. This amazing book contains the records of what Sarah has seen, heard, and learned during her divine visits to Heaven and Hell since November 2013. She wrote every detail, trusting in the Word of God. This has really ministered to me in a powerful way.

Words cannot describe how much I have been touched and blessed by her story, how biblical her revelations are and how God was gracious to grant her such revelations when she was praying with her whole body and spirit for at least 5-6 hours every day.

Although she may not be perfect before the Lord, He used her to give us a vision of hope of eternal life in Heaven that is in line with the Bible.

I strongly believe that this testimonial book will be used powerfully to minister to all the readers, no matter where they are in their faith journey.

I recommend this book, earnestly hoping that many will read it and believe that Heaven is real and gain hope for eternal life. To God be all the glory! Hallelujah!

John Park (park111151@hotmail.com)
Head Pastor of Chung-Ang Mission Church
39th President of Southern California Pastors Committee
Honorary Ph.D. from USC

Recommendation Letter

I first met Pastor Sarah Seoh on November 1, 2013.

It was truly by God's grace that I we met. I have no doubt that God is the One who connects people together and that nothing happens by accident. It was through a phone call with a pastor that I got to know about Pastor Seoh for the first time. I noticed that Pastor Seoh was as pure as a young lamb, striving hard to live each day with integrity. Although I was in Korea while she was in America, we began to talk very often through kakao talk.

We talked about Heaven and Hell as well as the ministries we were called to do. She would also share with me about her visits to Heaven and Hell and God's revelations to her each day, and we would discuss what we should do with these divine encounters and revelations. For example, when God continuously gave her revelations about a war in

Korea, we prayed together fervently for the nation. We didn't know what to do about it, how we should pray, or how we should let people know about these revelations from God.

I am confident that God has partnered Pastor Seoh and me for His Kingdom ministry. We also discussed and prayed how we could let more people know about Heaven and Hell so that one more soul may be saved.

I also believe that the part where God confirmed to Pastor Seoh that the human microchip implant is indeed the mark of the beast – 666 – is very helpful to know because there is a strong controversy going on about this and it is important that we accept what God has said.

I pray that this book will not be just another testimonial book, but that it would be used to help you open your spiritual eyes and take you to the place of repentance. I also pray in the name of Jesus that even though the time may come when the world will force us to receive the mark of the beast, that we will be strong enough to reject it and choose to follow His ways until the end. Hallelujah! I give praise to God who has once again revealed Himself to us through Pastor Seoh.

Pastor Woon-Kwon Baek
Evada Prayer Mountain

CONTENTS

INTRODUCTION

How I got to see Heaven and Hell

I am currently in my ninth year serving as the head pastor of a small church in Los Angeles, California. In obedience to the Lord's leading, I have also been serving as the director of the LA New Person Spiritual Training Center for four years. Since God is the Head of our churches, we as His servants should always remain humble before Him. And we should do our best to serve the people whom the Lord brings into our lives until He returns.

While I was serving the Lord, I had a growing desire to see Heaven and Hell. While I did open-air evangelism for ten years in LA, my passion for lost souls and my hunger for God began to grow stronger. If only God would reveal to me Heaven and Hell, I felt like I could be a better messenger for Him. So I began to pray, *Lord, please show me Heaven and Hell...* I longed for it so much that I started listening to various people's testimonies about their visits to Heaven and Hell. I then came across a pastor who had prayed for seven years, asking God to show him Heaven and Hell. So I prayed, *Lord, please show me Heaven and Hell... even if it requires me to pray for seven years.*

After a little while, I randomly got to talk on the phone with a pastor who had gone to Heaven and Hell in the past. I asked him what he had seen in Heaven, and what happens to our body when we go to Heaven. Then it happened. While I was still talking to him on the phone, my spirit was suddenly lifted out of my body and transported to Heaven. God saw my deepest longing and my earnest repentance that in the midst of a phone call with His anointed servant, and God lifted my spirit to show me Heaven and Hell. That was my first visit to Heaven and Hell. By God's grace, I got to see Heaven and Hell continuously.

At first, I couldn't believe it was really happening. But as time passed and the more I saw Heaven, God confirmed it to me in a way that only I could understand. Every single detail is written in this book. For example, God would tell me about some of the supernatural spiritual experiences I have had in the past; in other cases, He would let me meet some of the spiritual forefathers to ensure me I was really in Heaven. Indeed, during my visits to Heaven, I got meet many spiritual forefathers. I was really blessed and honored to have been given the chance to talk with them. Oh, how I long to see them again when I go to Heaven for eternity!

I can boldly say that the spiritual world really exists. Heaven and Hell are indeed real. If we repent and earnestly long to see the spiritual realm, God will reveal it to us. I never asked God to show me Hell, but He did. He showed to me very vividly the various places where the non-believers end up going. I believe that there is a problem within us if we are not able to see the spiritual realm because it really exists. If we sincerely repent before God and turn from our sinful ways, our spirit will be able to see the spiritual side since we are spiritual beings.

Some may say that God only reveals it to specific people, not to anybody. I am not sure about this. What I know for sure is that I had truthfully repented and pursued my longings, and God opened the doors for me to see. However, there had been another incident 18 years earlier.

I was praying in tongues on a prayer mountain from midnight to 5 AM along the ridge. I remember God trying to open the doors of Heaven right above my head, but I stopped Him. I was afraid. I was afraid of becoming arrogant if I saw Heaven. So I refused to see. But surprisingly 18 years later, I had a growing desire to see it. And thankfully, He allowed me to see both Heaven and Hell when I was ready.

Heaven initially looked black and white; but the more I saw it, everything began to appear in natural colors and I was able to see more clearly. God delights in those who sincerely repent. If you don't fully repent, or if there are any impure thoughts or sin within you, you will not be able to see Heaven and Hell. You have to pray for at least five to six hours, to cleanse yourself again and again. I didn't do this in order to see Heaven and Hell; this was what my normal prayer life looked like. And in order to see Heaven and Hell, I had to turn from the ways that were not pleasing to the Lord. I then found myself going to Heaven and Hell almost every day, and I started writing down everything I saw. And because God wanted me to, I ended up writing this book. This book is Volume One, in which I have written everything in chronological order. By the time this book gets published, I will be preparing Volume Two. The second book starts off with the revelations that God has given me in Heaven regarding the Korean War, which I had never even thought of before.

Without a doubt, we are now living in the end times, and Jesus is returning. We ought to prepare for His second coming and also keep our faith until the end. It would also be better if we could be taken at the rapture as His brides on the day of His return. I believe that God showed me Heaven and Hell because He has a specific message for all of us. I give all the glory to Him, who is coming soon!

"I am the Alpha and the Omega," says the Lord God, "who is and who was and who is to come, the Almighty." (Revelation 1:8)

PART I
Testimony of Heaven and Hell

1

My First Visit to Heaven and Hell
(11/1/13)

Jesus was the first One to come out to greet me (at first, I couldn't really see His face; but my spirit just knew He was Jesus. As days went by, I was able to see His face more clearly).

Jesus and I went to the house of the Apostle Paul. Paul wasn't very tall; in fact, he was quite short in stature. We went inside Paul's house, and the three of us sat around the table. Then I asked Paul how he was able to share the Gospel in the midst of all the sufferings he had gone through. And I asked him if that is how I should live on earth. I was very impressed with myself for asking the latter question. When I asked this question, Jesus gently grinned.

Instead of giving me an answer, Apostle Paul quietly stood up from his seat, approached me to give me a hug.

As he was giving me a warm embrace, I could feel his heart saying, "You do exactly that."

Oh Lord.....

2 Corinthians 11:23-27

"Are they servants of Christ? I am a better one—I am talking like a madman—with far greater labors, far more imprisonments, with countless beatings, and often near death. Five times I received at the hands of the Jews the forty lashes less one. Three times I was beaten with rods. Once I was stoned. Three times I was shipwrecked; a night and a day I was adrift at sea; on frequent journeys, in danger from rivers, danger from robbers, danger from my own people, danger from Gentiles, danger in the city, danger in the wilderness, danger at sea, danger from false brothers; in toil and hardship, through many a sleepless night, in hunger and thirst, often without food, in cold and exposure."

Afterwards, Jesus and I went to the house of David. David had a brown beard and was wearing a Roman soldier outfit with a sword in the side. As we walked into his house, numerous people in white robes were standing in two long rows to welcome us. At the moment, I was extremely curious who these people were. However, it suddenly dawned on me that these were the hundreds of falsely charged people who had followed David for years after years when Saul was chasing after David. These people were in Heaven. They probably came to know the Lord while following David all those time. David must have shared with them about the Lord whom he had personally encountered. And here they were, together in Heaven. Hallelujah! Hallelujah!

I later had a chance to ask David to confirm who these people were, and I was right.

1 Samuel 22:1-2

"David departed from there and escaped to the cave of Adullam. And when his brothers and all his father's house heard it, they went down there to him. And everyone who was in distress, and everyone who was in debt, and everyone who was bitter in soul, gathered to him. And he became commander over them. And there were with him about four hundred men."

Considering this was my first visit to Heaven, I got to see quite a lot of things.

I even got to meet Mary, the one who gave birth to Jesus. Mary was extremely beautiful. I still see her every time I go to Heaven; but when I saw her for the first time, I don't know why but I tried to kneel down before her. So the angel beside me raised me up and told me not to and added that Mary is not someone to be worshiped.

Deuteronomy 5:7

"You shall have no other gods before me."

This was such an awkward moment. It wasn't that I worshiped Mary while I was on earth, but it was so strange that my knees uncontrollably tried to kneel before her presence. I can't help but think that the Lord has intentionally allowed this to happen to let people know that Mary is not a subject to be worshiped. I praise Him for giving such confirmation.

Then the scene shifted. I suddenly found myself placed in a vast wilderness. I felt some chills and all of a sudden, I began to see some glimpses of hell.

I don't know how this was possible. One minute I was in Heaven, and now I was seeing Hell.

Then I saw a naked man, running for his life; but a snake that was about 30 cm thick coiled around the man's waist and pulled him to the ground. Then a devil's minion severed the man's abdomen into two parts. The parts that were cut gained back their flesh, but another servant of the devil came and struck the man's abdomen with spears repeatedly.

At that very moment, I thought to myself, *What has the man done to deserve such torment?* Then the answer was revealed to me in my mind. *Aha! He had committed adultery.*

A naked woman suddenly appeared. This was the woman he had committed adultery with. The chamber, with walls that were all reddish, looked very narrow and good for only one person to stay. There was another devil's minion standing in the corner with a spear, who appeared to be the one in charge of tormenting the woman. And there as well was a snake that was about 30 cm thick.

Matthew 18:8-9

And if your hand or your foot causes you to sin, cut it off and throw it away. It is better for you to enter life crippled or lame than with two hands or two feet to be thrown into the eternal fire. And if your eye causes you to sin, tear it out and throw it away. It is better for you to enter life with one eye than with two eyes to be thrown into the hell of fire.

2

Encounter with the Father of Faith, Abraham, and his son, Isaac

(11/4/13)

It was 8:20 in the morning. Inside the carriage that came to pick me up to go to Heaven, Jesus was sitting with an open Bible. I couldn't believe the Lord was inside the carriage. I quickly sat next to him, and in a split second, we were already up in Heaven. As we entered the castle, the Lord said to me, "There is a place we must go," and He took me through the clouds. I was curious where He was taking me, but soon I figured that we were heading to the house of Abraham. When we arrived, there was a pond in the garden; and from the pond, a sparkling carp that had scales of orange and blue in color leaped to my hand and spat out a reddish gemstone. Abraham led Jesus and me to his house, and we met Sarah, Abraham's wife, inside the house. Their son, Isaac, joined us very shortly as well. All five of us sat down in a beautiful round table, drank some reddish juice. There also was a tray of fresh grapes before us.

I asked Abraham, "How were you able to fully trust in God's promise and without a second thought, ready to sacrifice your own son?" There was a long silence until Abraham finally opened his mouth. "That's exactly what faith is..." I was able to sense the depth and width of his unwavering faith that God's Words are always true and steadfast. *Aha! I see....*

I then asked Isaac how he was able to go up to the altar without rebelling when he could have simply pushed his old man and run away.

Genesis 22:9
"When they came to the place of which God had told him, Abraham built the altar there and laid the wood in order and bound Isaac his son and laid him on the altar, on top of the wood."

He replied, "That's what faith is all about."

Hallelujah! It was not just Abraham, but Isaac too had such a solid faith. Isaac believed that he would be raised to life again. After our conversation, I told them that I desire to have such faith as well.

Sarah Seoh

Hebrews 11:17-19

"By faith Abraham, when he was tested, offered up Isaac, and he who had received the promises was in the act of offering up his only son, of whom it was said, 'Through Isaac shall your offspring be named.' He considered that God was able even to raise him from the dead, from which, figuratively speaking, he did receive him back."

Considering he was very young, probably a teenager, at the time, it is truly amazing that Isaac laid down on the altar because he had faith in the Word of God. Just like his father Abraham, Isaac also believed that God was going to fulfill His promises of granting numerous offspring to Abraham, even if it meant raising himself (Isaac) from the dead.

Genesis 15:2-5

"But Abram said, 'O Lord GOD, what will you give me, for I continue childless, and the heir of my house is Eliezer of Damascus?' And Abram said, 'Behold, you have given me no offspring, and a member of my household will be my heir.' And behold, the word of the LORD came to him: 'This man shall not be your heir; your very own son shall be your heir.' And he brought him outside and said, 'Look toward heaven, and number the stars, if you are able to number them.' Then he said to him, 'So shall your offspring be.'"

I believe that it was both Abraham's and Isaac's faith on the altar that moved the heart of God. Therefore, we can see that after this incident, God blessed Isaac wherever he went without him having to go through severe hardship. Isaac personified Jesus Christ and Abraham personified God the Father who sent His Son to be crucified. *O Lord!*

After I heard Abraham and Isaac's responses to my questions, I told them how much I wanted to have faith like theirs. Hallelujah!

Lately, I have been having doubts in my mind whether this whole thing of riding a carriage and visiting Heaven was really happening because it was still somewhat surreal to me. But I believe that the Lord allowed me to meet Abraham and Isaac to reenact a spiritual experience I had had in the past while I was praying. God used this way to confirm to me that everything that was taking place right now was true. Hallelujah!

In the past, there was a time when I was praying in desperation at a church, asking God to help me surrender myself fully to Him. *God, please teach me what surrendering really means, then I will do it for You because You said that You use people who have surrendered their lives to You.*

I was crying out to God wholeheartedly when I suddenly saw a young man dressed in white walking towards me and sitting down at the stairs before me. In an instant, I knew He was Jesus. I could see Him even with my eyes closed.

He was holding a Bible, and he started turning the pages. I somehow knew He was turning the pages to Genesis, where it talked about Abraham. Strangely, the two sides of the pages were blank.

On one page, Jesus wrote "I" and on the next page, He wrote "saac." At that very moment, I had a divine understanding that surrendering one's self to God is having the heart of Abraham when he sacrificed Isaac on the altar. If we were in his position, we would have prayed to God to kill us instead of having to sacrifice our own child. But Abraham obeyed with no second thought. He had a heart that was fully surrendered to God. God uses such people who obey His commands as His vessels.

God has confirmed me today in such a special way that I was seeing Heaven for real.

O Lord, Hallelujah. Thank You. No longer will I doubt.

3

Ariel Castro in Hell

(11/5/13)

A naked man came to sight all of a sudden. The devil's minions were
pulling the man's mouth wide apart from both sides with long wooden
sticks. I couldn't imagine how painful it must be for him. His mouth
seemed to be tearing apart from the torture. Again, this man was
naked. Then the devil's servants pulled out his arms and legs all at
once, tearing his skin apart. The strange thing was that the man's
bones and ligaments stayed attached to his body, even while the skin
ripped apart. The next thing I saw was the devil's minions chewing
and eating the ripped skins. It was a horrible sight. The moment I was
wondering who this man was, it was revealed to me instantly in my
mind that he was Ariel Castro, the man who had been charged for

the Cleveland kidnapping case, which had alarmed the whole world in February 2013. He had kidnapped and held three young women (Gina de Jesus, Michele Knight, and Amanda Berry) as captives for more than a decade in his own house. He was a vicious criminal who had sexually and psychologically abused the girls while locking each of them in the basement, first floor, and second floor. I was seeing this man being harshly tormented in hell.

4

My house in Heaven

(11/7/13)

As soon as I returned to Heaven, I got on a golden boat by the riverside with the Lord. Some beautiful swans on the river looked at us and warmly greeted us. Then the Lord led me to my house in Heaven.

There was a beautiful, cozy bed inside my house. At the far end of the living room to the right, there was a luxurious bathtub. The mirror and the washstand were really beautiful as well. In the spacious living room, there was a piano and a dining table that was all made of pure gold. *Wow!* I was completely struck with awe. *A piano made of gold. A long rectangular dining table and chairs, all made of gold. I couldn't believe it.*

Just the day before, I had actually visited the house of one of my church members. The house was grand and really gorgeous, which made me a little bit envious. I wondered what it would be like to live in such a mansion. Their piano and their dining table especially caught my attention. Compared to the member's house, my house (on earth) seemed small and dull. Having thought of this just the day before, how timely it was for the Lord to show me my house in Heaven with the golden piano, table, and chairs! I was so grateful. I didn't even ask Him to show me my house.

It then occurred to me how worthless everything is on earth.

1 John 2:15-17

"Do not love the world or the things in the world. If anyone loves the world, the love of the Father is not in him. For all that is in the world—the desires of the flesh and the desires of the eyes and pride of life—is not from the Father but is from the world. And the world is passing away along with its desires, but whoever does the will of God abides forever."

I realized that everything of this world is only momentary.

As I came out of the front door of my house, there was a garden where beautiful yellow flowers were blossoming in one corner. And several carps were hopping along the pond saying, "Our master is here! Our master is here!" They recognized me even if I hadn't said a word. I gently stroked one of the carps that leaped up.

5

Jesus, my Groom

(11/10/13)

When I went up to Heaven, there were four angels dressed in white who looked like the servants from the ancient time of the Joseon Dynasty. I noticed they were extremely fast in motion, and that their facial features looked quite bizarre. Their faces were flat, but the shapes of their faces were triangular. They swiftly took me on a ride through a floral sedan chair, which the Korean brides rode in older times. I didn't know where they were taking me to, but soon I was brought to a riverside where other angels were waiting for me. They took me to the waters and gave me a clean bath. Then the angels dressed me with a fine linen cloth, in which the top was covered with a tulle fabric. On top of this cloth, they dressed me with a Korean traditional jacket that the brides would wear in the old days. I was extremely curious what was going on and why they were dressing me with these.

The extremely fast angels, who looked like servants from the Joseon Dynasty, took me to the floral sedan chair again for another ride. I arrived at a banquet hall. As soon as I got off the sedan chair, I saw the Lord waiting for me to take me for a dance. Surprisingly, He was waiting for me, fully dressed in the Korean traditional costume that the grooms wore in the past. He was wearing a white traditional lower garment, and an upper garment, topped with a blue jacket, all of Korean traditional clothes. He was even wearing the traditional hat that the grooms used to wear. And just as the grooms did traditionally, he was waiting for me, the bride, to get off the floral sedan chair. My heart was so moved and my eyes got watery. I was overwhelmed by His love. I was so full of joy that I cried, and we danced in the banquet hall endlessly.

When we were dancing on the stage of the banquet hall, I found myself dressed in Western-style garments. I was in a ballet dress, while Jesus was wearing a suit. I cannot dare to describe into words how happy I felt when I was dancing with the Lord. My heart was overflowing with pure joy.

Song of Solomon 2:2-7

"As a lily among brambles,

so is my love among the young women.

As an apple tree among the trees of the forest,

so is my beloved among the young men.

With great delight I sat in his shadow,

and his fruit was sweet to my taste.

He brought me to the banqueting house,

and his banner over me was love.

Sustain me with raisins;

refresh me with apples,

for I am sick with love.

His left hand is under my head,

and his right hand embraces me!

I adjure you, O daughters of Jerusalem,

by the gazelles or the does of the field,

that you not stir up or awaken love

until it pleases."

I was His bride, and He was my Groom.

6

What happens in Heaven when we condemn others

(11/12/13)

When I arrived in Heaven, I was already in front of God's throne. Before His presence, my whole being fell prostrate to the ground. Then my condemning heart towards OOO came to light.

At that moment, the angels who were standing beside me laid over me a large glass box. The next thing I knew, I was placed outside and stuck inside the glass cube. I felt like I was confined in a prison cell that was small enough for only one person to fit.

Then I was reminded of a specific passage from the Bible that talked about the people bringing before Jesus a woman who had committed adultery and said, **"Teacher, this woman has been caught in the act of adultery. Now in the Law Moses commanded us to stone such women. So what do you say?" (John 8:4-5).** Jesus, in response, bent down and wrote something on the ground with His fingers then said, **"Let him who is without sin among you be the first to throw a stone at her" (John 8:7b).** At this, the people dropped the stones and left one by one, from the oldest to the youngest. In the end, it was only the woman and Jesus who were left. At that moment, Jesus spoke to the woman. He said, **"Neither do I condemn you; go, and from no on sin no more" (John 8:11b).**

I recalled this passage of Jesus' forgiveness to the woman. I realized the fact that I too am a sinner before God; therefore, I have no right to condemn anybody. I couldn't help but confess my sin before the Lord inside the glass cube. *Lord, I confess my sins. I have condemned OOO. Please forgive me. I won't condemn again.*

While I was desperately and earnestly confessing my sins, the angels approached me and removed the glass cube away from me. Hallelujah! I was so surprised.

That is right. When we condemn someone on earth, we become confined in a glass cube in the spiritual world, and this blocks us from having a direct fellowship with the Lord.

Afterwards, more Scriptures came to mind.

Even though God has forgiven us with ten thousand debts, we are often so hard to those who only owe us a tiny portion of debt. When the Master sees how we have been treating our debtors, I realized how natural it is for God to place His wrath upon us. Hallelujah! *Lord, I won't condemn others again.*

Matthew 18:35

"So also my heavenly Father will do to every one of you, if you do not forgive your brother from your heart."

Therefore, when we condemn others, we create a barrier between God and ourselves.

Isaiah 59:1-2

"Behold, the LORD's hand is not shortened, that it cannot save, or his ear dull, that it cannot hear; but your iniquities have made a separation between you and your God, and your sins have hidden his face from you, so that he does not hear."

Lord, please help me that I may no longer condemn others....

7

Encounter with the Apostle Peter

(11/12/13)

Just like the former times, I was taken swiftly to heaven through a floral sedan chair. Earlier I hadn't been able to see the faces of the angels who were guiding me and driving the carriage, but I could now see their faces.

My outfit always changes right before arriving in Heaven. I always find myself wearing a golden crown that is not too heavy and an elegant white dress that is embellished with light-colored sparkling jewels here and there. And every time I enter Heaven, the Lord is waiting to greet me at my right side. He was there today as well.

What was out of the ordinary that day was that numerous angels were moving around very hastily in Heaven? *What was happening?*

I was curious but at that very moment, a sight of an angel who just held a knife to cook a huge carp caught my attention. Then Jesus took me to go somewhere. He took me to a banquet hall. There were many round tables that were neatly arranged, and each table looked large enough to accommodate about 12 to 13 people around. The tables were all made of pure gold and were covered with a fine white cloth. Jesus and I sat next to each other in one of the round tables and enjoyed a meal. Interestingly, whenever I thought of a specific food or dish that I wanted to eat, an angel would bring to our table exactly that food. When I thought to myself that I wanted to have a cheesecake, an angel brought to me a plate of cheesecake. What an extraordinary experience. We also drank something that looked like raspberry juice from a nice glass.

While we were still enjoying our meal, Jesus suddenly ordered the angels to bring the fish dish they had been cooking. The angels brought the dish right away, and Jesus and I began to eat it; but to tell the truth, I couldn't really tell what it tasted like.

Throughout the banquet, I couldn't help but wonder why Jesus had brought me here. After we had left the banquet hall, Jesus spoke as if He had read my mind. He said that He wanted me to know that we can eat, drink, and even enjoy banquets in Heaven.

Revelation 21:4

"He will wipe away every tear from their eyes, and death shall be no more, neither shall there be mourning, nor crying, nor pain anymore, for the former things have passed away."

Then He took me by the clouds to a higher place. I could see green trees at the edge of the horizon, and some buildings that were sparkling with colors like that of jade. As I was questioning myself where that place must be, the word "Peter" just penetrated to my mind very strongly. At that moment, I just knew that we were heading towards the house of Peter. The next second, we were already in front of Peter's house. As we entered into the front door of his house, Peter (who seemed very busy working on something inside the house) stopped what he was doing and ran outside to greet us. He greeted us as if he were expecting us. I could easily sense Peter's clumsy character through his gestures and facial expressions. Three of us were very happy and we sat down around a table.

Apparently, Peter wasn't wearing a crown. He had a dark, curly hair with long facial features and big, round eyes. He was also wearing white. I was wearing a white dress too, with a golden crown.

But all of a sudden, I felt ashamed before Jesus and Peter for wearing a crown because not even Jesus' top disciple was wearing a crown. I felt like I didn't deserve to be wearing it. But Peter knew what I was thinking, and I felt like he was saying to me to my heart, "I feel comfortable not wearing a crown."

And then at that moment, I suddenly saw a crown at the far end corner of a room. I soon realized there were about six or seven crowns that were lined up orderly inside. *Oh wow!*

Then my eyes caught the attention of a large picture frame while I was looking around the living room. As soon as I saw the picture frame, I was very astonished. The picture was portraying Peter sinking in the water because he was afraid when he saw the wind, while he was walking on the water towards Jesus. In the picture, Jesus quickly comes to Peter and extends His hand to help Peter out.

This huge picture was hanging in Peter's house. But the reason I was so surprised to see this was because I have the exact same picture that I have deliberately framed in my room for more than a decade. I would never have expected to see this very picture in Heaven, let alone in the living room of Peter's house! It was unbelievable. I had this picture frame hanging in either my room or my living room for over ten years because I didn't want my lack of faith to sink me down. I wanted to remind myself that the moment I doubt, I will end up falling like Peter did. It was just amazing to see this picture again in Heaven and at Peter's house.

Matthew 14:28-31

"And Peter answered him, 'Lord, if it is you, command me to come to you on the water.' He said, 'Come.' So Peter got out of the boat and walked on the water and came to Jesus. But when he saw the wind, he was afraid, and beginning to sink he cried out, 'Lord, save me.' Jesus immediately reached out his hand and took hold of him, saying to him, 'O you of little faith, why did you doubt?'"

I had always remembered what Jesus had said to Peter, "O you of little faith, why did you doubt?"

As the three of us were sitting around the table, a specific memory suddenly popped into my head. It was back in 1997 when I had gone to Grace Prayer Mountain. I believe Jesus had brought this to my mind for a purpose.

At Grace Prayer Mountain, I was being trained to pray in tongues every night for five hours, from midnight to 5 AM, and to read the Bible for at least five hours no matter what during the daytime. After a few days of training, I was reading the Old Testament in a small trailer when I felt the Lord asking me, "Do you love Me?"

I remembering replying, "Lord, it is because I love You that I got fired from my work for evangelizing, and it is because I love you that I came here to the prayer mountain to prepare myself to go to the path You are leading me to."

But I strongly felt the Lord asking the same question again, "Do you really love Me?" So I replied, "Lord, You know that I love You."

But again He asked, "Do You really love Me?" I am not sure if it was because He asked me the same question three times despite my answers, but when He asked me the third time, I burst into tears and cried out, "Lord! You know that I love You!" I kept crying. Then I heard Him say, "Then follow Me."

After some time had passed, I was appalled at what I found while reading through the book of John in the New Testament. I had no idea that Jesus had already asked Peter the exact same question He had asked me, according to John 21. Back in the prayer mountain, where He asked me the question three times, I had a very shallow understanding and knowledge of the Bible. I didn't know that Peter too had received the exact same question three times in a row. I couldn't believe the same account that I experienced has already been recorded in the book of John.

I was recalling this while I was sitting around the table with the Lord and Peter. Then Peter spoke up. He said, "I was beside the Lord at that time (when the Lord asked you three times)."

Somehow I just knew exactly what he was talking about even if he didn't say the details. As I heard him say this, I was so touched that my physical body began to shake and I began to cry. *How awesome it is that Peter was with Jesus when He asked me those questions.*

John 21:15-22

"When they had finished breakfast, Jesus said to Simon Peter, 'Simon, son of John, do you love me more than these?' He said to him, 'Yes, Lord; you know that I love you.' He said to him, 'Feed my lambs.' He said to him a second time, 'Simon, son of John, do you love me?' He said to him, 'Yes, Lord; you know that I love you.' He said to him, 'Tend my sheep.' He said to him the third time, 'Simon, son of John, do you love me?' Peter was grieved because he said to him the third time, 'Do you love me?' and he said to him, 'Lord, you know everything; you know that I love you.' Jesus said to him, 'Feed my sheep. Truly, truly, I say to you, when you were young, you used to dress yourself and walk wherever you wanted, but when you are old, you will stretch out your hands, and another will dress you and carry you where you do not want to go.' (This he said to show by what kind of death he was to glorify God.) And after saying this he said to him, 'Follow me.'

"Peter turned and saw the disciple whom Jesus loved following them, the one who also had leaned back against him during the supper and had said, 'Lord, who is it that is going to betray you?' When Peter saw him, he said to Jesus, 'Lord, what about this man?' Jesus said to him, 'If it is my will that he remain until I come, what is that to you? You follow me!'"

Then Jesus said to Peter, "Peter, open your heart and show Sarah." I didn't understand what Jesus meant by that. But I found myself asking Peter, "Peter, when you were imprisoned and chained between two prison guards, how were you able to sleep not knowing when they will execute you?" (I later knew that the Lord was the One who led me to ask this question).

Then all of a sudden I had flashbacks of scenes that showed how much Peter loved Jesus. Peter really did love Jesus dearly. That is why on the night Jesus was taken, Peter was able to claim that he would follow Him wherever He went. Even when everybody thought Jesus was a ghost when He was walking on the water, Peter was the first one to respond to Jesus when He said, "Take heart; it is I. Do not be afraid." Peter said, "Lord, if it is you, command me to come to you on the water."

Even when Jesus revealed himself to the disciples by the Sea of Tiberias, Peter was the first one to dive into the waters to meet Jesus. While I was thinking about these incidents and how much Peter did love Jesus, Peter said, "The thought of dying tomorrow really brought me joy."

As he spoke these words, I was able to clearly understand what he was saying. Peter had followed Jesus for three years, has witnessed the death and resurrection and even the ascension of Jesus! It was clear to me that Peter was not afraid of death because then he would be with

Jesus forever in Heaven. Although it was a simple truth, it shocked me because I had never regarded death as a joyful thing in the past. *Aha! This is exactly why Jesus had told Peter to open his heart and show me something. Jesus knew I would have these questions.* That is right. I now realized that death should be regarded as a glorious thing. Hallelujah! I praise God for revealing to me a new perception about death.

Romans 14:8

"For if we live, we live to the Lord, and if we die, we die to the Lord. So then, whether we live or whether we die, we are the Lord's."

8

Hell, where the people who don't believe in Jesus go

(11/13/13)

In the morning, I got to witness three scenes from Hell. Just as on the ordinary days, I went up to Heaven riding on a golden carriage. As soon as I arrived there, Jesus was standing there but I sensed something was very strange and different.

When I got off the carriage, in an area a bit lower than the ground I was standing on, I could see a panorama of countless number of people's heads very closely packed together. It looked like the old Korean matchboxes that had matchsticks jam-packed inside, only it was real human heads, billions of them that were literally filling the whole horizon. While my gaze was still fixated to this view, I noticed they were all heading downwards. It is hard to explain, but I was able to see a close-up of these people's heads, and then I was somehow able to see the depths of where these people were. They were in an extremely dark and deep place. In an instant, I felt that I was in Hell. I was so scared that I held the edge of Jesus' gown with all my strength.

Then I began to see people who were going through extreme suffering. Jesus and I were actually standing at the verge of a fire pit in Hell. At the opposite end were people who were being burnt by the furious fire. The people inside the fire were screaming and crying their heads off.

And my eyes caught another horrifying sight. At the edge of the blazing fire, naked people were running around with all their might trying to avoid the fire. The weird thing was that while the people were running to escape the fire, the fire was actually chasing after the people. The people could not run too far because the devil's minions were standing in one line, waiting to strike the people's belly with their spears. Their spears were all pointed towards the people's stomachs.

I could feel what was going through the people's heads at that moment. Somehow I was reading the minds of the people who were trying to run away from the blazing fire. My heart sank as I could feel and read what the people were feeling and thinking, "The fire is too hot, but if I go run away, the spears are waiting for me. What should I do? Should I choose to get struck by the spear? Would that be a little better than the fire?" While these people were debating between the two terrible options, they were already being poked and struck by the spears and thrown back to the blazing fire.

I couldn't breathe nor stand watching this dreadful sight. I was completely horrified and began to groan. Just then, Jesus took me out from the pit of hell and we went up. From the top, I could see something that looked like a cliff where people were coming out through a dark hole that was smaller than the size of my house front door. From that hole, people were coming out, one by one, bound to hell.

I could see a number of these of dark holes just from where I was standing. In each of these holes, the devil's minions were standing by and whenever a person would come out and wonder, "Where am I?" or realize they were arriving in Hell, the devil's minions would push these people to the fire pit. So everything took place very instantly. The area of the cliff was only spacious enough for one or two people to stand. And right below the cliff was the blazing fire. It just took one push for a person to fall into the furious fire.

In between the holes, more of the devil's minions who seemed to be of a higher rank were looking out to make sure the lower-rank minions were doing their job well. This was very frightening to see. Nobody had a choice here.

Jesus then spoke to me, "Will you still proclaim the Gospel?" This hell was where the unbelievers were bound to come. I began to cry. I felt so bad for those who were coming to hell, and the thought of the people coming here because they didn't believe in Jesus made me so sad.

Revelation 20:15

"And if anyone's name was not found written in the book of life, he was thrown into the lake of fire."

Then I thought to myself that I no longer wanted to see Hell because I couldn't bear watching the people who were suffering and being tormented. So I said to Jesus through my mind, *Lord, I don't want to see Hell anymore. I don't want to see it.*

There was silence for a while and then all of a sudden, I couldn't see anything. Then a man began to come to sight. I didn't ask him to show me something nor did I expect to see anything. The man's left eye didn't have an eyeball. It was grooved and there was blood streaming down. Somehow I immediately knew that the devil's minion was the one who took out his eye. Nobody told me, but God revealed it to me through my mind.

Another devil's minion was trying to aim his spear towards the man's remaining eye to pull it out as well. The two minions were grabbing and twisting the man's hands very tightly behind him, not letting him move. Another minion was poking the man's stomach with the spear, and still another minion was eating the skins that were skewered in the spear.

I asked the Lord in my mind, "Lord, what has this man done to deserve such pain and suffering?" Then I was able to know that he was a man who had a lot of hatred and had not worked off his grudge when he was on earth. This was revealed to me naturally right away.

Matthew 18:23-35

"Therefore the kingdom of heaven may be compared to a king who wished to settle accounts with his servants. When he began to settle, one was brought to him who owed him ten thousand talents. And since he could not pay, his master ordered him to be sold, with his wife and children and all that he had, and payment to be made. So the servant fell on his knees, imploring him, 'Have patience with me, and I will pay you everything.' And out of pity for him, the master of that servant released him and forgave him the debt. But when that same servant went out, he found one of his fellow servants who owed him a hundred denarii, and seizing him, he began to choke him, saying, 'Pay what you owe.' So his fellow servant fell down and pleaded with him, 'Have patience with me, and I will pay you.' He refused and went and put him in prison until he should pay the debt. When his fellow servants saw what had taken place, they were greatly distressed, and they went and reported to their master all that had taken place. Then his master summoned him and said to him, 'You wicked servant! I forgave you all that debt because you pleaded with me. And should not you have had mercy on your fellow servant, as I had mercy on you?' And in anger his master delivered him to the jailers, until he should pay all his debt. So also my heavenly Father will do to every one of you, if you do not forgive your brother from your heart."

Then against my will, I was once again exposed to Hell. I found myself with Jesus in a muddy ditch that had some water-like fluid flowing. I soon figured it was blood, not water. I could tell it was blood even though it was extremely dark.

We both crossed the ditch; then before our eyes in the opposite side, we saw a man being chopped into pieces. His arms and legs were amputated with a saw and thrown all around. The remaining parts of the body, the head and the body, were then taken to the straw cutter where the head was cut and dropped to roll over and over. Then the other minions of the devil picked up the amputated arms and legs and carried them on a stretcher.

It was truly a gruesome sight. The blood that had been flowing initially was from this very place. I then wondered who these people were. Then it was revealed to me in my mind that they were the people who have murdered and even chopped people during their lifetime. They have killed and mutilated people's bodies, but now they had to suffer this way eternally.

2 Corinthians 5:10

"For we must all appear before the judgment seat of Christ, so that each one may receive what is due for what he has done in the body, whether good or evil."

9

My house in Heaven

(11/13/13)

After seeing Hell for a while, the same angels guided me back to Heaven through the same carriage. Surprisingly, the place where Jesus and I arrived was my house. In the garden of my house, there was a pond where carps were leaping out of joy to see me. In return, I gave honor to Jesus and thanked Him. Before we entered the house, there were two angels with wings and both of them were standing in the front gate to greet us. Then we entered the house and sat across one another in the long, rectangular dining table that was made of gold.

The Lord was holding a book that had records of what I had done for Him, while I had a copy version of that book (I later found out that this was my "Book of Memories," but at the time, I was only informed that this book contained the records of all the things I had done for the Lord in the world). Jesus looked through the whole book. He was reading all the things I was currently doing and all the mission work I would do in the days to come. I too looked through the copies. Then Jesus led me to the storage room for weapons in the house. Inside the storage room were loads of swords, knives, spears, and other weapons that were piled up, and an angel was arranging them by hanging one by one on the wall in an orderly way.

Then Jesus spoke. He said, "These are the swords, spears, and arrows of the fire of the Holy Spirit that you shall use to fight against Satan and his minions. I will give all of these to you." Hallelujah! Then He dressed me in an armor suit, armed me from top to toe, and handed me the furious sword, spear, and arrow of the Holy Spirit. Heavily loaded and armed, I came back down. Hallelujah!

Let me pause for a moment. The furious sword, spear, and arrow of the Holy Spirit may sound weird to some people. But this is something that happened in the spiritual realm, so I have come to understand it now. I also now understand why Jesus was looking through the Memory Book when we visited my house in Heaven. He wanted to encourage me to work, being fully armed and equipped spiritually. Just as when we cast out demons in Jesus' name, the demons will come out from the person. I was reminded of God's Word.

Matthew 12:28

"But if it is by the Spirit of God that I cast out demons, then the kingdom of God has come upon you."

Thus, I now fully understand why it was so important to be fully armed with the weapons of the Holy Spirit before coming back to the world. The Lord had spiritually armed me.

Hallelujah!

10

Second visit to the Apostle Paul's house (11/15/13)

There were so many more angels with wings than usual in Heaven. Even when Jesus was taking me somewhere through the clouds, I noticed that some of these angels were riding with us. I didn't exactly understand what was happening. About seven of these angels were standing in a row next to me, and all of them looked very happy and excited. I couldn't stop wondering why these angels were riding with us because it was usually just Jesus and me.

As we flew through the clouds, a large castle came to sight in a distance. Just when I was questioning where that could be, it was supernaturally revealed to me that it was the house of Paul. I didn't know why we were going to Paul's house again. Right before we entered into Paul's house, all of the angels who accompanied us flew away. None of them went in the house with us.

Before I go on, let me take the time to record what Paul's house was like. The outer form of the house looked like a castle with pointed rooftops like the ones we normally see in fairy tale books or cartoons. The color of the roofs was purple-like, and the remaining part of the castle was a very pretty turquoise-like color.

After we entered into the house, Jesus, Paul, and I sat around the table. Then all of a sudden, the incident where Paul had cast out demons from the fortune-teller came to my mind. Somehow I was then informed supernaturally in my mind that the Lord was going to give me the spiritual gift and the power to cast out demons. Hallelujah!

Even the incidents of Paul raising Eutychus, who had fallen from the third floor, from the dead, and of the sick being healed simply through touching Paul's handkerchief, came to my mind. And likewise, I was informed that I would be granted the gift of healing as well. Hallelujah! I was so grateful. We then stacked our hands together and prayed. They were imparting their gifts to me.

Then, Jesus and I came out from the house of Paul and rode on the clouds. Interestingly, the seven angels with wings returned to accompany us again. But this time, each of them was holding a jewel box. Somehow I knew that the jewel boxes were for me.

I realized that the reason Jesus had taken me to Paul's house was to impart on me all of his spiritual gifts.

Acts 19:12

"So that even handkerchiefs or aprons that had touched his skin were carried away to the sick, and their diseases left them and the evil spirits came out of them."

11

Lord of Mercy, with flowers and animals of precious gems and jewels

(11/15/13)

As I entered in the Gates of Heaven, my outfit changed. I usually would be wearing a golden crown, but today, I was wearing a different crown that was embellished with diamonds. And I was also wearing a new, white dress.

Jesus greeted me on my right side as He always did. My heart was overjoyed. My love for Him soared up and I couldn't contain my joy and love for Him, which was expressed through tears. I cried and my heart was telling Him how much I had missed Him. I was just so happy to be in such a loving relationship with the Lord. I felt that He shares such a loving relationship with every single believer.

Jesus and I were walking on a golden road when I found that my one hand had a white glove on. Right then, a bird flew to me and sat on my gloved hand and greeted me. I wondered why I was wearing a white glove since I had never worn one in Heaven before. But I realized that it was an act of love from Jesus. He knew ahead that a bird would fly to me and sit on my hand, so he put a glove in my hand in advance so that I wouldn't be flustered. Or He could have commanded the angels to put on a glove in my hand so that He could call on the bird to come to me. Whatever it was, I was touched at how detailed Jesus' love was.

Jesus and I then went to a flower garden that was made of precious stones and jewels. There was a golden road in the middle of the flower bed. The flowers looked real but when I looked closely, they were flowers that were made of gems and jewels with delicate care and detail.

To our left was a beautiful royal azalea blossom with fresh green leaves. There were roses with petals that were red at the edges and orange towards the center; some were pink. There were also flowers that were purple, yellow, and others even had a mixture of red and white in them. A butterfly then flew to me and rested on my hand that had the glove on. It was a beautiful butterfly that had mixtures of orange and red. To the right of us was a golden field of reeds. Oh what a beauty it was! The reeds were like golden grains of rice.

Then Jesus and I went to a zoo that was made of precious gems and jewels. A gigantic elephant came to greet us. This elephant looked like a clear precious jewel of light pink in color. There was also a gentle-looking lion and a leopard, as well as purple monkeys. I also saw a peacock that spread its beautiful wings and a deer that was made of gold.

In the midst of such beauty and perfection, the scenes shifted unexpectedly. I was in Heaven thus far, but without warning, I was seeing Hell. And before my eyes were people being tormented in the blazing fire. I also saw a snapshot of the people suffering, where the fire became like a needle, poking and stinging their entire bodies with severe pain.

And suddenly I saw iron bars before my eyes. I initially saw one chamber surrounded by iron bars; then I saw multitudes of the kind all laid out in a row. In each chamber, there was one person imprisoned. Outside the chambers, the devil's minion was crushing one person at a time into a tub and thrashing the person as if he was milling. I could see the intestines bursting forth as a result of this. Then I saw another devil's minion who was standing by, sticking the intestines onto his skewer and munching on them. *Lord, what kind of people end up here where there is so much pain and agony?* The moment I had this question in my mind, I knew supernaturally that these were the people who have lived a life full of lies in the world.

As I moved forward, I saw an iron pot over a blazing fire, and people were being thrown into the pot to be boiled. And somehow I just knew that these people would later be eaten by the devil's minions. I also knew that these people were gluttons who were very selfish and did not know how to share with others during their lifetime.

12

Receiving my calling in Heaven

(11/16/13)

Today was special in that two angels with wings were blowing golden trumpets on both sides of me, while I was going to Heaven on the golden carriage. Upon arrival, I saw Jesus wearing a white gown that was too bright for me to look at. He was taking me somewhere, and a winged angel in white followed us, carrying a large, golden tray.

We arrived inside a building that was made of gold. No angels could be found in there. It was just the Lord, me, and the angel who was carrying the large, golden bowl. I suddenly noticed Jesus holding a scroll in one hand. As He unrolled the scroll, I saw a calligraphy that read, **"I, Jesus, am the one who was and is and is coming."**, The Lord said to me, "Share this to the people." At the moment, I heart was so touched and moved. *God was giving me a calling...*

Revelation 1:7-8

"Behold, he is coming with the clouds, and every eye will see him, even those who pierced him, and all tribes of the earth will wail on account of him. Even so. Amen. 'I am the Alpha and the Omega,' says the Lord God, 'who is and who was and who is to come, the Almighty.'"

Then Jesus said that in the large tray were the teardrops from my eyes while I prayed. The angel then poured them out onto a long jar that was made of precious stones that had a color of something in between peach and pink. As the teardrops were being poured into the jar, they changed into flat and round gemstones, filling the jar from the very bottom. The jar was very beautiful and the length of it was longer than one meter.

Afterwards, we headed to my house in Heaven. The angel, who was holding the jar of teardrops, came along with us. There were beautiful flowers in the garden. The carps in the pond leaped up even higher today than usual and rejoiced, saying, "Our master is here. Our master is here." One of the carps leaped to my hand and spit out a bluish gemstone for me.

I also saw the angel, who had accompanied us, placing the jar of gemstones right near the pond. Then beautiful colors of the gemstones brightened up the house and made it even more radiant. I also found out that this very angel was actually one of the two angels who guard the front door of my house. I knew this because when we arrived home, there was only one angel standing at the front door, and the angel who came with us quickly went and stood by the front door.

I realized it was one of these two angels in my house who brought my teardrops in a golden tray then transferred the teardrops to the jar then brought it to my house. When Jesus and I entered my house, I told Him how much I missed my earthly father. In a short while, my earthly father suddenly came to my house. My father marveled at my house and seemed very pleased. Then he left.

13

First conversation with the angel who was guiding me

(11/17/13)

I was lifted up to Heaven after I earnestly prayed for repentance. Before I go on, it is important that I explain what I had repented for because no matter how much I tried to go to Heaven, God didn't let it happen until I repented about this particular sin. It was for my ungrateful heart about God's revelation to me of Heaven and Hell. Even though I did desperately long to see Heaven, after visiting both Heaven and Hell several times, I began to think it was not that difficult to see them after all and my heart was no longer as grateful as it should have been. However, God revealed this to me and desired that I should repent.

God was in a way disciplining me for my ungrateful and arrogant heart because no matter how much I prayed and tried to go to Heaven and Hell, nothing was happening. He had to deal with my heart first because I was taking His grace and divine revelations for granted. I deeply and earnestly repented for my unfaithful heart and asked for His forgiveness.

Then I tried again to see Heaven. At that moment, the angel in the golden carriage that came to take me to Heaven looked directly to my face and said, "Come on. The Lord is waiting." That was my first conversation with the angel who always drove me to Heaven. I got on the carriage and went up. Indeed, the Lord was waiting for me. My feelings for Him were no longer that of a bride, but more of a young child. He was like a Father. As soon as I saw Him, I said, "Papa, please forgive me." Papa patted me on the head and said it was all right.

2 Corinthians 6:1-2

"Working together with him, then, we appeal to you not to receive the grace of God in vain. For he says, 'In a favorable time I listened to you, and in a day of salvation I have helped you.' Behold, now is the favorable time; behold, now is the day of salvation."

Just as on my last visit, I was wearing a white dress and a diamond crown. Only this time, the Lord and I were not moving around on clouds. We were riding on something that looked like a gigantic clam shaped like a boat. The colors were somewhat pinkish and medium-toned scarlet, and the outside had patterns that looked like rays of light. *What's going on?*

It was an amazing feeling though because I have never ridden this way before. Just as the clams of the sea, the inside of this "clam boat" was very smooth and silver-white in color. Jesus asked, "Is there anywhere you want to go?" Without hesitation, I replied, "The Sea of Glass, Papa." "Alright let's go!" And off we flew on the clam boat. I felt like Jesus was rewarding me because I have been convicted and repentant of my sins of not having been grateful. Jesus already knew I wanted to go to the sea of glass before He even asked me, and I believe that is why He had prepared the clam boat instead of the clouds.

When we arrived there, our clam boat went just slightly above the water level. It just felt like riding on an ordinary boat. The Lord had prepared this clam boat in advance because He knew where I wanted to go. Hallelujah. Amen. Amen. I realized that Jesus was making my travel plans in Heaven in advance, and this really touched me.

Revelations 15:2-4

"And I saw what appeared to be a sea of glass mingled with fire— and also those who had conquered the beast and its image and the number of its name, standing beside the sea of glass with harps of God in their hands. And they sing the song of Moses, the servant of God, and the song of the Lamb, saying,

'Great and amazing are your deeds,

O Lord God the Almighty!

Just and true are your ways,

O King of the nations!

Who will not fear, O Lord,

and glorify your name?

For you alone are holy.

All nations will come and worship you,

for your righteous acts have been revealed.'"

The waters of the sea of glass were very calm and peaceful. I asked the Lord, "Are there any fish that live in the sea of glass?" And just as I was asking this question, a large orange fish that was swimming in the waters came to my attention. The fish then suddenly made a high jump to greet me. Hovering in the air above Jesus and me was an angel, who was dressed in white, blowing the trumpet. Riding on a clam boat with Jesus on the sea of glass, with an angel blowing the trumpet above us, and an orange colored fish leaping around us – it truly was an amazing moment.

We were there for a quite a while. Afterwards, Jesus and I flew to another place on clouds, leaving behind the clam boat on the sea of glass. The next place we went was where the river of life and the tree of life were. I was certain the fruit was peach, but it was as big as a child's head. I picked the fruit from the tree and ate it.

I then made a request to the Lord: "Lord, would you show me the things you have not shown to others?" He then took me to the bank in Heaven. Dressed in armors and helmets and holding spears, two armed soldiers were standing in front of the bank just like security guards. I was curious why these men were fully armed and looked as if they were guarding the bank, for this was Heaven, after all. But I felt like the Lord made it to appear to look so that I may understand this place bears the image of a bank in Heaven.

When we entered in the building, I was very amazed at how big and beautiful it was. The whole place was made with marble; but once I took a closer look at the marble, I realized that it was actually all gold. Instead of tellers sitting in different partitions, there were two or three angels "working" there but with no partitions.

As soon as Jesus entered the bank, He commanded the first angel in sight to bring in my bankbook. Once the angel came out with my bankbook, I was so surprised that it looked so beautiful and was even made of gold. The bookmark as well was made of gold. At that very moment, I suddenly understood the calculation method of Heaven. Then I was reminded of the story of the widow with two copper coins.

Luke 21:1-4
"Jesus looked up and saw the rich putting their gifts into the offering box, and he saw a poor widow put in two small copper coins. And he said, 'Truly, I tell you, this poor widow has put

in more than all of them. For they all contributed out of their abundance, but she out of her poverty put in all she had to live on.'"

Then I mentioned about the pastor who had visited Heaven and Hell to Jesus. I said, "Lord, I heard that he had seen the History Museum of the Creation of Mankind. Can you show it to me? I also heard from him that there are various levels in Heaven. I want to see that too." Jesus then replied, "Let's do this, slowly." Then I came back down.

14

Visit to the History Museum of the Creation of Mankind

(11/18/13)

One of the angels who came to pick me up on the golden flower carriage with two white horses said, "The Lord is waiting" as soon as I saw them. Hallelujah! I was so excited. As soon as I saw the Lord in Heaven, I wanted to hold His hand and that is exactly what I did! In fact, I asked Him to hold my other hand. He then held both of my hands and spun me around and carried me to His back. Hallelujah! Oh, how great that feeling was! I was filled with so much joy that I couldn't contain it.

After He put me down, we rode on the clouds together. Unlike the previous times, there was a bench for two persons on the clouds we were riding on. So Jesus and I sat on the bench and flew, while two winged angels dressed in white blew the trumpets. We flew on the clouds for quite a while until we came across a large round roof underneath us that was gray and dark greenish in color.

From our view from atop, the roof was round with a spiral pattern that started from the center. The moment I asked, "What is that?" we were already in the aisle where the entrance to that building was. There was also an angel in white who was there to greet us. As we went inside, I was stunned by the extensiveness and the fancy picture frames on the walls as well as the extremely high ceilings. I immediately knew that this was a museum. I had just asked about the History Museum of the Creation of Mankind the day before, and I knew the Lord had remembered and thus brought me to that very place today. I also noticed several people looking through the works of art in the museum.

I watched the people until Jesus came to me. At that very moment, something I had never noted before caught my attention. I noticed that the Lord's glory was surrounding Him where He was standing, and everybody greeted by saying "To God be the glory!" As Jesus came in the building, His light of glory came in as well and spread out from the edge of His clothes to His surroundings. When the people who were looking at the artwork felt His glorious light, they all recognized that it was the Lord and turned around to see Him. It seemed as though the Lord's holy light shone only at certain times because it was the first time that I had seen it.

I asked the Lord, "Where should I start?"

He then led me to the stairs that was heading down. There were 3 floors down, and we went to the lowest floor. The first piece of art displayed there was the drawing of the time God created the heavens and the earth. In the next painting, I saw Adam and Eve. The two were very beautiful and glowing. But after they had sinned, their faces changed. They looked ugly and different. Their faces were overshadowed with darkness.

Genesis 3:6~11

"So when the woman saw that the tree was good for food, and that it was a delight to the eyes, and that the tree was to be desired to make one wise, she took of its fruit and ate, and she also gave some to her husband who was with her, and he ate. Then the eyes of both were opened, and they knew that they were naked. And they sewed fig leaves together and made themselves loincloths.

"And they heard the sound of the LORD God walking in the garden in the cool of the day, and the man and his wife hid themselves from the presence of the LORD God among the trees of the garden. But the LORD God called to the man and said to him, 'Where are

you?' And he said, 'I heard the sound of you in the garden, and I was afraid, because I was naked, and I hid myself.' He said, 'Who told you that you were naked? Have you eaten of the tree of which I commanded you not to eat?'"

At that very moment, I saw the snake that had tempted Eve. The head was a snake, but it had four legs.

Aha! The snake had originally walked in four legs!

Genesis 3:14~15
"The LORD God said to the serpent,
'Because you have done this,
cursed are you above all livestock
and above all beasts of the field;
on your belly you shall go,
and dust you shall eat
all the days of your life.
I will put enmity between you and the woman,
and between your offspring and her offspring;
he shall bruise your head,
and you shall bruise his heel.'"

Then I saw the painting that portrayed Cain and Abel. The thought of Cain killing his brother Abel out of jealousy disturbed me that I didn't want to see the painting anymore. I told the Lord, "I will look at it again next time." Jesus replied, "Okay" and we left the place by riding on the clouds.

Afterwards, a scene from Hell was shown to me. I saw a spirit who was soaked in a deep mud puddle and coming out in deep agony. I first saw his hands come up, followed by his head. He didn't have eyes; instead the mud was filling in where his eyes should have been and was streaming down his face. Then I saw him imprisoned behind iron bars.

Outside the prison, I could see one of the devil's minions bringing a red-hot instrument and violently stabbing it to the spirit's abdomen area. I could hear and even smell the skin burning before my eyes. I cried out, "O Lord!" in my mind. And I asked the Lord quietly in my mind why this person was being tormented as such. The Lord revealed to me that this man was a swindler and used to deceive others.

15

Visit to the children's playground in Heaven
(11/19/13)

When I went up to Heaven, the Lord welcomed me and said, "My beloved bride, come on." Seeing the Lord brought so much joy to me! As I took a walk with the Lord, I noticed a multitude of baby angels flying and following us right above our heads. I wondered why there were so many baby angels who were following us today.

Then we came across something that looked like a tunnel. And the baby angels went before us in line and flew into the tunnel. Jesus and I went in the tunnel as well. The floor inside the tunnel was white, but the top and the sides were very dark. *Where is this heading? Could it be hell? It can't be... This can't be leading to hell with all these baby angels alongside.*

Just when I was thinking these thoughts, I saw a bright light at the end of the tunnel, and we eventually were able to come out to that bright place. Oh Hallelujah! Before my eyes was a large playground for young children. It then became clear why those baby angels were following us. Numerous children were playing in the playground. There were swings, slides, and something like a merry-go-round. Mary came and spoke with Jesus. She was very beautiful. The Lord then said that He had to leave soon with her. So I bid them farewell and came back down.

16

Encounter with Daniel

(11/20/13)

Before I got on the golden carriage that transports me to Heaven, the angel who usually escorts me told me that the Lord was waiting for me. As soon as I rode the carriage, I had already arrived in Heaven. But this time, I was led directly to a castle. The castle was made of gold, and it was very grand and elegant. Numerous angels were standing in both ends, and the Lord was sitting at a golden throne. I fell on my knees before His feet and cried. I had missed the Lord so much and it was being revealed through my tears again. The Lord looked at me and grinned. Then suddenly, the sound of music started to spread around and the music perfectly described my heart for Jesus – how much I had longed for Him and missed Him. However, interestingly, I could not hear the music, but I could tell that the music was echoing around. Hallelujah!

After a short while, the Lord and I left the castle. I noticed again how colossal the castle was. The Lord and I then rode on the clouds and went to the house of Daniel. When we arrived, the three of us sat around the table. Daniel was a handsome young man with light-colored hair.

I told Daniel that I had a question for him. The Lord had told Daniel ahead of time to answer my question. So I started asking him some questions: "Daniel, how were you able to pray continuously when you knew that it would lead you to the lion's den?" Daniel replied, "I prayed three times a day for my people. I couldn't stop praying for them. And I was not afraid of men." When I heard this, I was immediately reminded of the Bible verse, "What can man do to me?"

Hebrews 13:6
"So we can confidently say,
'The Lord is my helper;
I will not fear;
what can man do to me?'"

Galatians 1:10

"For am I now seeking the approval of man, or of God? Or am I trying to please man? If I were still trying to please man, I would not be a servant of Christ."

Daniel was not afraid of men because God was so much greater and important than men. He also added, "When I found out that I was going to be thrown into the lions' den if I prayed openly, the Lord said to me, 'Do not be surprised. Do not be afraid for I am with you.'" Hallelujah! That is why Daniel didn't stop praying three times a day even though he knew he would be thrown into the lion's den. Hallelujah!

Daniel 6:10-13

"When Daniel knew that the document had been signed, he went to his house where he had windows in his upper chamber open toward Jerusalem. He got down on his knees three times a day and prayed and gave thanks before his God, as he had done previously. Then these men came by agreement and found Daniel making petition and plea before his God. Then they came near and said before the king, concerning the injunction, 'O king! Did you not sign an injunction, that anyone who makes petition to any god or man within thirty days except to you, O king, shall be cast into the den of lions?' The king answered and said, 'The thing stands fast, according to the law of the Medes and Persians, which cannot be revoked.' Then they answered and said before the king, 'Daniel, who is one of the exiles from Judah, pays no attention to you, O king, or the injunction you have signed, but makes his petition three times a day.'"

And Daniel said, "So I ended up going into the lions' den, but the lions were all sitting down and behaving so well. Although those lions had been starved for days, they were very calm and still until I was taken outside."

Daniel 6:19-24

"Then, at break of day, the king arose and went in haste to the den of lions. As he came near to the den where Daniel was, he cried out in a tone of anguish. The king declared to Daniel, 'O Daniel, servant of the living God, has your God, whom you serve continually, been able to deliver you from the lions?' Then Daniel said to the king, 'O king, live forever! My God sent his angel and shut the lions' mouths, and they have not harmed me, because I was found blameless before him; and also before you, O king, I have done no harm.' Then the king was exceedingly glad, and commanded that Daniel be taken up out of the den. So Daniel was taken up out of the den, and no kind of harm was found on him, because he had trusted in his God. And the king commanded, and those men who had maliciously accused Daniel were brought and cast into the den of lions—they, their children, and their wives. And before they reached the bottom of the den, the lions overpowered them and broke all their bones in pieces.

****Before Daniel had been thrown to the den of lions, the Lord had sent forth His angel in advance to shut the lions' mouths. That is why the lions were sitting down quietly even when Daniel was thrown before them. And when Daniel was released from the den, the angel of the Lord unzipped the mouths of the lions. Hallelujah.

I told Daniel that I wanted to receive his gift of interpreting dreams. Then Daniel placed his hand over mine, and the Lord placed His hand over Daniel's; and they prayed that it would be done so. Hallelujah. I thanked the Lord for allowing me to meet Daniel today.

As a side note, I want to describe how Daniel's house looked like. I actually saw his house just last night. There was huge patch of grass in front of his house. His house was very "modern," a castle that looked like the National Assembly. It was gigantic and simply amazing.

(This building looks very similar to the house of Daniel.)

17

People who have destroyed families through adultery in Hell

(11/20/13)

I had a feeling my second visit would be in Hell. And my instincts were right. As soon as I went up, I saw scenes from Hell. A man and a woman, both naked, were standing. And another man and woman were hanging from a cliff. Their hands were tied up somewhere on the cliff. The devil's minions were viciously spanking their buttocks with a sharp rod, and blood started to stream from their bottoms.

Then one minion suddenly pulled off the man's private part with all his might and began eating it. Another minion brought a long iron stick and thrust it into the woman's private part. The devil's minions were performing these actions repeatedly.

I couldn't stop but wonder what these people had done to be suffering such a torture. As I was thinking about this, it was revealed to me that the woman was married with two children, and the man next to her was single. Unfortunately, these two people had committed adultery with one another, which ended up breaking apart the woman's family.

18

The pastor who had passed away a month earlier in Heaven

(11/21/13)

As soon as I arrived in Heaven, the Lord took me to very bright place far away. It was the throne of the Lord. Multitudes of angels greeted us from all corners as I entered into the castle with the Lord. The Lord sat at His throne, and I was about to fall prostrate to the ground before Him as a sinner. But the Lord sat me down to the left of His throne. It was where the angels were standing, and I was sitting in the front that was closest to the Lord. As I was sitting there, I told the Lord that I wanted to see Pastor OO Lim. Then a young man with a slightly long face entered in. He looked a bit rough, and he was wearing a white gown that was not exactly white or bright. He was also not wearing a crown.

****Before I go on, allow me to share a little bit about Pastor Lim.

Just the other day, I received a call from Korea. It was a pastor who had heard that I was visiting Heaven and Hell. The pastor said, "Pastor Seoh, a pastor whom I know had recently passed away. I was wondering if you could check if he went to Heaven because his wife is extremely curious. Would you ask the Lord when you go to Heaven?" I heard that this late pastor had gone through many trials while he was alive. His church didn't have many members; he also had some family issues, etc.

The pastor who called me insisted so desperately that I decided to ask the Lord about this pastor once I go to Heaven. And the Lord indeed showed me this pastor. But since I had never met this pastor before, I wasn't completely sure whether he was the right man or not. So when the pastor from Korea called me again, I first asked him, "Can you tell me what the late pastor looked like?" Instantly, the pastor began by saying, "His face is a bit long and..."

At that very moment, I knew I had seen the right man and said, "Oh! Then I did see him in Heaven! That's exactly what I thought when I first saw him." The pastor was filled with joy knowing that Pastor Lim was in Heaven.

Matthew 7:21-23

"Not everyone who says to me, 'Lord, Lord,' will enter the kingdom of heaven, but the one who does the will of my Father who is in heaven. On that day many will say to me, 'Lord, Lord, did we not prophesy in your name, and cast out demons in your name, and do many mighty works in your name?' And then will I declare to them, 'I never knew you; depart from me, you workers of lawlessness.'"

Then Pastor Lim disappeared, and the Lord and I got on the clouds and arrived at the History Museum of the Creation of Mankind. I could see the aisle and an angel who were waiting to greet us. The floor of the museum was all in marble that was turquoise in color. It was so beautiful.

As soon as I entered the museum, the Lord and I had some clashing opinions in our minds. I was personally interested about the end times, of the things that will take place in the last days. However, for whatever reason, the Lord would not let me see it. I just felt it all by heart and I also somehow understood why He wouldn't show it to me. The reason for his refusal was because I had pride in my heart and a desire for fame, when that should not be the case. Thus, if the Lord were to show me about the things that will happen in the end times, I would be conceited and proud for knowing something more than others. This is why the Lord kept it from me.

We ended up going to the floor that showed the beginning of the New Testament – from the birth of Christ, to His public ministry, and to His ascension. There were three more floors above the level where we were in. In the floor above us, there were writings about the seven churches from the Book of Acts to Revelation; but I was not yet allowed to clearly see these writings.

19

Encounter with the woman the Bible depicts as a "sinner" in Heaven

(11/22/13)

I was crying in the golden carriage on my way to Heaven. This was because I had missed the Lord so much. Upon my arrival, I noticed that the Lord seemed taller than usual and that He was dressed a long, white robe.

I fell under his long gown and wept. (I later realized that the Lord had appeared taller than usual and had dressed in a long robe because He knew ahead that I would fall under His dress and weep).

The Lord said, "My child..." and comforted me. At the time, I was clothed in a white dress and was wearing a crown. Then we both took a walk on a golden road for a long time. I just wanted to be by His side. I loved Him so much!

As we were walking together, a golden eagle flew towards us and took us for a ride. It felt incredible. The golden eagle flew very high and flew until we saw the sea of glass; it then turned around and dropped us off at the History Museum of the Creation of Mankind.

As soon as we entered the door to the museum, I begged the Lord to allow me to clearly see the drawings that were displayed in that floor. Instantly, I was able to vividly see the painting that was right in front of me. The drawing portrayed a woman who was a sinner, crying at the feet of Jesus and wiping His feet with her hair. As I was looking intently at the drawing, that very woman appeared next to me. She had large eyes and a round face. She was also dressed in a white dress and was wearing an ornamental fabric over her head. Before we knew it, Jesus and I were at the woman's house.

Luke 7:36-38

"One of the Pharisees asked him to eat with him, and he went into the Pharisee's house and reclined at the table. And behold, a woman of the city, who was a sinner, when she learned that he was reclining at table in the Pharisee's house, brought an alabaster flask of ointment, and standing behind him at his feet, weeping, she began to wet his feet with her tears and wiped them with the hair of her head and kissed his feet and anointed them with the ointment."

Three of us were sitting around the table that was dark grayish in color with little white spots, embedded with precious stones. We all had noodles with soup, and the meal was very nice. I couldn't believe I was eating noodles in Heaven!

Then the Lord opened the golden treasure box that was on the table, and He took a large diamond golden ring and gave it to me. The ring was so beautiful. I was curious as to why He was giving this golden ring to me, and then it clicked.

Two days earlier, I went to Chinatown to evangelize and I happened to go in the street where the jewelry stores were packed. I then went inside a jewelry store and pretended shopping around because I had to give out the evangelical flyers. I even tried on some rings that I liked, but the prices were extravagant. The average price ranged from 7,000 to 15,000 dollars! *Wow. So expensive!*

I was thinking to myself that I couldn't afford it and even felt a bit jealous towards those who were able to buy and wear them. The price of the rings depended on the size of the diamonds in them, and most of the rings were gold. After trying on some rings, I told the seller that I would come back again next time and left the evangelical flyer before coming out.

The Lord knew my heart, and He gave me a diamond ring that surpassed all other rings I had seen. I felt bad and a little embarrassed before Him because I felt like He caught me envying others who were wearing such rings. I was ashamed. *Lord, I'm sorry and thank you for this beautiful gift. Hallelujah.* He knew ahead and prepared it in advance to give it to me.

When I told Him, "Lord, I heard that many people repented during the revival worship that Pastor Baek had led," His eyes welled up into tears as He was eating the noodles. And He said, "I was there." Hallelujah!

1 John 2:15-17

"Do not love the world or the things in the world. If anyone loves the world, the love of the Father is not in him. For all that is in the world—the desires of the flesh and the desires of the eyes and pride of life—is not from the Father but is from the world. And the world is passing away along with its desires, but whoever does the will of God abides forever."

20

Encounter with Solomon in Heaven
(11/22/13)

I went up to Heaven twice this morning. More angels came out to greet me. As soon as I arrived, they were giggling and chatting to one another. I didn't know what was going on, but one of the angels carried a pen and a notepad and came along as Jesus and I were about to take off through the clouds. I realized that this angel was the "scribe" who was in charge of recording things.

Then we arrived at the History Museum of Creation of Mankind. The angel followed us to the museum; and as we entered in, a handsome young man came approached us. He had a long, white fabric over his shoulders that fell to the ground. I didn't know who he was at first; but soon, I figured he was Solomon.

So it happened naturally that we visited the second basement floor where the works of Solomon were displayed. In that floor, there were pictures of God's Temple that Solomon had built and of Solomon giving thanks to God in front of the people after the Temple had been completed.

I Kings 8:18-20

"But the LORD said to David my father, 'Whereas it was in your heart to build a house for my name, you did well that it was in your heart. Nevertheless, you shall not build the house, but your son who shall be born to you shall build the house for my name.' Now the LORD has fulfilled his promise that he made. For I have risen in the place of David my father, and sit on the throne of Israel, as the LORD promised, and I have built the house for the name of the LORD, the God of Israel."

I Kings 8:26-30

"Now therefore, O God of Israel, let your word be confirmed, which you have spoken to your servant David my father. But will God indeed dwell on the earth? Behold, heaven and the highest heaven cannot contain you; how much less this house that I have built! Yet have regard to the prayer of your servant and to his plea, O LORD my God, listening to the cry and to the prayer that your servant prays before you this day, that your eyes may be open night and day toward this house, the place of which you have said, 'My name shall be there,' that you may listen to the prayer that your servant offers toward this place. And listen to the plea of your servant and of your people Israel, when they pray toward this place. And listen in heaven your dwelling place, and when you hear, forgive."

Another picture presented the scene of Solomon being a wise judge over two mothers and a baby, when both women kept claiming the baby as their own.

I Kings 3:16-28
"Then two prostitutes came to the king and stood before him. The one woman said, 'Oh, my lord, this woman and I live in the same house, and I gave birth to a child while she was in the house. Then on the third day after I gave birth, this woman also gave birth. And we were alone. There was no one else with us in the house; only we two were in the house. And this woman's son died in the night, because she lay on him. And she arose at midnight and took my son from beside me, while your servant slept, and laid him at her breast, and laid her dead son at my breast. When I rose in the morning to nurse my child, behold, he was dead. But when I looked at him closely in the morning, behold, he was not the child that I had borne.' But the other woman said, 'No, the living child is mine, and the dead child is yours.' The first said, 'No, the dead

child is yours, and the living child is mine.' Thus they spoke before the king.

"Then the king said, 'The one says, "This is my son that is alive, and your son is dead;" and the other says, "No; but your son is dead, and my son is the living one."' And the king said, 'Bring me a sword.' So a sword was brought before the king. And the king said, 'Divide the living child in two, and give half to the one and half to the other.' Then the woman whose son was alive said to the king, because her heart yearned for her son, 'Oh, my lord, give her the living child, and by no means put him to death.' But the other said, 'He shall be neither mine nor yours; divide him.' Then the king answered and said, 'Give the living child to the first woman, and by no means put him to death; she is his mother.' And all Israel heard of the judgment that the king had rendered, and they stood in awe of the king, because they perceived that the wisdom of God was in him to do justice."

I noticed that only pictures that depicted Solomon's good work for God were displayed in the museum.

Below the paintings were doors attached to the walls that could be opened. One you open it, you could see divisions of small shelves that were filled with green-leathered books decorated with gold in the center. These books were the records of all that Solomon had done in his life.

We then returned to the main floor and went up one floor. There, we could see the things that were described in the Book of Acts. At the end of that floor, there were the letters that were written for the seven churches.

21

The children whom the Lord
cares for in Heaven

(11/22/13)

As usual, I went up to Heaven riding on a golden carriage. The Lord
then took me to His throne. While He sat on His throne, I sat at his
left side where my chair was in front of the standing angels. It was
a special seat made for me. On both sides of the Lord's throne were
multitudes of angels standing in a line.

After sitting down for a while, scores of children dressed in white
came in to where we were. They were each holding a basket of flowers
and as they entered, they were sprinkling the flower petals before the
Lord, the angels, and me. I could tell that the Lord delighted in these

children very much. Still resting on my chair, I wondered who these children could be. Then the answer supernaturally was given me that these were the children who were discarded before birth by their parents. But since the parents have sincerely repented of their sin, the Lord was taking care of these children in Heaven. I felt so sorry for these children. I checked the children one by one just in case my child was there. But I was confirmed that my child was not among them. My heart still ached.

All of the children covered their body in white, and they were all wearing a short white skirt with long, white socks. So from a distance, it appeared as though they were dressed in all white. The children were extremely vibrant and looked really happy. After the children left, the Lord and I left the place as well.

Matthew 19:14
"But Jesus said, 'Let the little children come to me and do not hinder them, for to such belongs the kingdom of heaven.'"

22

My very own child in Heaven

(11/23/13)

As I was trying to hop onto the golden carriage bound for Heaven, I noticed a little boy sitting inside. He was dressed in a traditional outfit that Korean babies normally wear on their first birthday. I sat right next to him. *Could this child be...my child?*

As I entered into the gates of Heaven, the Lord spoke to me, "This child is your child." The Lord was holding this child, but as soon as I got off the carriage, the boy came to me calling me, "Mom." My heart was deeply moved and overwhelmed with emotions. I held my boy for a long time and just savored the moment. Then the Lord told me that

I would be able to live with him when I come to Heaven for good. I couldn't believe it. I was filled with unspeakable joy.

When I had seen the children in short skirts come to the throne of the Lord yesterday, the Lord knew I was thinking about my child. He was so gracious to allow me to meet my son for a short while today. I was so thankful. The Lord truly knows everything. In Heaven, you don't even have to speak because you can communicate through your mind.

As I was holding my son, I thought I would be able to take him to my house. But then, a woman who was dressed in white with an apron came up and gently asked me for the boy. She then took him. She is probably the one who is taking care of my son in Heaven.

Then the Lord and I sat down in a long, pink chair and four angels came and carried the chair to take us somewhere else. The place we arrived was a beautiful flower garden. It was filled with dark reddish and orange flowers that were blooming amidst the fresh, green leaves.

There was another garden to the right as well. Suddenly, a frog that had a yellow and green skin and was as big as my fist came up to me and looked straight in my eyes, uttering, "Hi, Sara. Glory to God!"

The Lord and I took a stroll through the garden without speaking a single word. Just being with Him was more than what I could ask for.

23

Heaven's records, the place of repentance, and twelve gates of pearl

(11/23/13)

There I was in Heaven. The Lord knew how much I desired to be with Him. I couldn't contain my love for Him. His presence overflows my cup with joy.

We both took a walk along the seaside of the sea of glass. We rode the clam boat again which we had left on the sea last time. Jesus rowed the boat, and we talked for what seemed like hours on end.

I asked Him to show me the twelve gates of pearl. Without a single warning, we were already riding on the clouds and headed somewhere. All of a sudden, I saw a grand gate that was made of pearls and precious stones. I only saw a part of the gate, but I was ecstatic. It was just amazing. I somehow just knew supernaturally that this was the east gate. "Lord, who enters this gate?" The second I asked this question, it was revealed to me that the martyrs are the ones who can enter through this east gate.

The next place we went to was the place of repentance. Multitudes of people or spirits were on their knees. Upon our arrival, three to four angels who were working there came to greet us. It hit me for the first time that angels were working here. Among the crowds of spirits who were kneeling down, one particular spirit zoomed in before my eyes and was shown to me in a close-up. The spirit had his eyes closed and his lips firmly shut.

His face looked solemn and also seemed like he was in pain. I was curious as to why these people were here. At that moment, I supernaturally knew these people had believed in Jesus when they were living on earth but their lives were no different from the non-believers. They did not live according to the word of God. Thus, they did not choose the narrow path that led to Heaven and didn't even bother to remember what Jesus had done for them on the cross. Simply put, they were not serious about receiving the grace of God.

Just as it is written in the Book of Revelation, in the letters for the seven churches, these people were those who didn't fight for their faith, but instead had lived according to the desires of their flesh and had not eaten the flesh of Jesus nor drunk His blood as they should have. Therefore, although they had believed in Jesus, they had not repented of their sins but followed their flesh. I realized that such people who resemble the people of the church in Laodicea end up in this place.

Revelation 3:14-22

To the Church in Laodicea

"And to the angel of the church in Laodicea write: 'The words of the Amen, the faithful and true witness, the beginning of God's creation.

"'I know your works: you are neither cold nor hot. Would that you were either cold or hot! So, because you are lukewarm, and neither hot nor cold, I will spit you out of my mouth. For you say, I am rich, I have prospered, and I need nothing, not realizing that you are wretched, pitiable, poor, blind, and naked. I counsel you to buy from me gold refined by fire, so that you may be rich, and white garments so that you may clothe yourself and the shame of your nakedness may not be seen, and salve to anoint your eyes, so that you may see. Those whom I love, I reprove and discipline, so be zealous and repent. Behold, I stand at the door and knock. If anyone hears my voice and opens the door, I will come in to him and eat with him, and he with me. The one who conquers, I will grant him to sit with me on my throne, as I also conquered and sat down with my Father on his throne. He who has an ear, let him hear what the Spirit says to the churches.'"

Then, the Lord and I headed to the History Museum of the Creation of Mankind. The floor that we entered into displayed various historical accounts of the Lord, from His birth to His ascension to Heaven. On the floor above us, which I will call the first floor, there were accounts from the book of Acts and many more in the middle of the floor. At the farther end of the floor was the letter from the Lord to the seven churches.

I asked the Lord again, "Where are the books that hold records of what each individuals have done for You?" The Lord told me that this history museum only keeps the general records of how the Kingdom of God is being built and how the saved souls have received salvation. He added that the records of what individuals have done for the Lord are kept in a different place. He then took me to that place.

We arrived in a totally different place, where the records of every individual's life and acts are stored. It was a one-story, tile-roofed building that was very long and white. Flocks of angels in white dresses were hastily going around from door to door. They were all recording each person's life and deeds.

It now clicked to me that the Book which Jesus had been looking at in my house the other day was the book of records about my life and ministry. I was able to tell that there weren't many writings on my book. When I asked the Lord, "What should I do for You?" He replied,

"Be my witness. Share about me, Jesus, the One who was and is and will come soon." Hallelujah! Then I returned back to my home.

Revelation 22:12-13

"Behold, I am coming soon, bringing my recompense with me, to repay each one for what he has done. I am the Alpha and the Omega, the first and the last, the beginning and the end."

Revelation 20:11-15

Then I saw a great white throne and him who was seated on it. From his presence earth and sky fled away, and no place was found for them. And I saw the dead, great and small, standing before the throne, and books were opened. Then another book was opened, which is the book of life. And the dead were judged by what was written in the books, according to what they had done. And the sea gave up the dead who were in it, Death and Hades gave up the dead who were in them, and they were judged, each one of them, according to what they had done. Then Death and Hades were thrown into the lake of fire. This is the second death, the lake of fire. And if anyone's name was not found written in the book of life, he was thrown into the lake of fire.

24

A famous megachurch pastor who had passed away behind iron bars

(11/24/13)

It was another day in Heaven as usual. Once again, the Lord was there to greet me. We flew on the clouds to a place where a swarm of clouds had collected together. The clouds were bulging and spread out at the same time. *Why were all these clouds flocked together like this?* The moment I was thinking this it was revealed to me that these clouds were actually the means of transportation to get around places for the people in Heaven.

I then told the Lord that I wanted to sit down on a bench and just talk with Him. He said, "Okay," and took me through the clouds to a garden where there was a bench. The garden looked blurry, probably because I didn't pay close attention to it. All that mattered to me at the moment was the fact that I was with the Lord. But when the Lord tried to show me each flower in the garden, the colors and every detail of the flowers became very clear to my eyes.

I asked the Lord, "Lord, I want to see Pastor OOO." I said this because I had no doubt this Pastor was in Heaven. He led a megachurch and had also become very renowned for His huge ministry when he was on earth.

But to my surprise, the Lord's face suddenly became grim and creased with anger. His words were even more shocking: "He is not here."

"What? Then where..."

"Why do you want to see him?"

I became completely speechless. Then the Lord said, "He had taken away my glory."

All of a sudden, the scenes before me shifted, and right before my eyes was Pastor OOO. He was dressed in white but behind iron bars. He exclaimed, "Why do I have to be here? Why?!!! Ugghh... you don't want to come here. Even if you do the work of God, if you steal His glory, you will end up here like me. Don't come here. Don't come here!"

As I was watching him, I thought of the two great ministries for which he had been famous while he was alive on earth. He was well known for his ministries in Japan and his ministries through television and other media. He had certainly done marvelous things for the Lord, but in reality his own name had become higher than the name of the Lord.

I cried out, "O Lord! What should I do?" And then I was back in the garden, sitting on the bench with the Lord. I don't know if I had visited hell then returned to the garden, or whether I had just seen the scene from hell from where I was.

The Lord was weeping and murmuring, "My servants...." It was painful. My heart sank.

This happened between 9 and 10 PM. But for an hour and a half, my spirit was grieving continuously. Around 11 PM, I laid down in my bed to go to sleep; but I couldn't brush off the thought of Pastor OOO. My soul was distressed and very sad. At 1:30 AM, I was still up, still struggling to go to sleep.

No matter how much we do for the Lord, we should always remember our identity before Him and give all the glory to God. We, His servants, should always choose to increase His name and decrease ours.

Isaiah 42:8

"I am the LORD; that is my name;

my glory I give to no other, nor my praise to carved idols."

Luke 17:7-10

"Will any one of you who has a servant plowing or keeping sheep say to him when he has come in from the field, 'Come at once and recline at table'? Will he not rather say to him, 'Prepare supper for me, and dress properly, and serve me while I eat and drink, and afterward you will eat and drink?' Does he thank the servant because he did what was commanded? So you also, when you have done all that you were commanded, say, 'We are unworthy servants; we have only done what was our duty.'"

God's servants who claim to be doing God's ministries end up in the iron bars if they take away all the glory that is due God. Regardless of how successful our ministries are, we should always give back all the glory and praise to God who alone deserves it.

Note: I cannot say for certain whether the place where I have seen the pastor was Hell or in the so-called place of repentance or outside the castle. At this point, I can only testify what was revealed to me, that this pastor was not in Heaven and that he was confined in iron bars.

25

God speaks about VeriChip

(11/25/13)

Just as on the other days, I went up to Heaven. The first words of the Lord were, "It was hard, right?" I broke down and buried my face at the edge of the Lord's gown and bitterly wept. The Lord knew that I couldn't stop thinking about Pastor OOO all night. My heart still aches.

Then we both took a long stroll along the road that was engraved with golden stones. We walked and walked until we came to the end of it. We were actually standing on a cliff, where I could see the bottom of the cliff.

Oh my.... I was very surprised. Underneath the cliff was a huge city where countless number of houses and buildings were tightly packed. Instantly, it was revealed to me that this was the world.

Amazingly, I could see and understand all the different things that were going on in each of the buildings. Although the buildings were all covered with rooftops, I could visibly see everything that was going on inside. On one side, I could see people committing robbery; on another side, I could see people fighting in their homes; and in the opposite side, I could see people singing songs and worshiping God. As I turned to the other side, I could see some people preparing for war; while others were starving to death on the other side.

At that very moment, I felt that the omniscience and the omnipotence of God for He knew every single thing that was going on at the same time. Then out of the blue, I asked Him about VeriChip. It happened very randomly was definitely not something I had planned. "Lord, should I receive the VeriChip or not?" Then the Lord said, "You should not receive it." He continued, "Receiving the VeriChip is the same as selling your soul to technology and to modern civilization."

The Lord also revealed to me that once you receive it, the Holy Spirit will leave you. He said that our souls ought to live by following His voice, but the moment we receive the VeriChip, we will be controlled by technology instead of God.

I asked Him further, "Lord, is VeriChip the mark of the beast, 666?" He replied, "That is right. Tell the people not to receive it. **But look over there. Can you see those places that have already begun implementing it? The number of people who receive it will** gradually increase; and eventually, people will be forced to get it for they won't be able to buy and sell without it."

"Oh no. Then I will not receive it. I won't."

I believe the Lord showed me the world because He knew I would ask about the VeriChip. To put it more exactly, I believe He had put that question to my mind and made me ask about it, so that I will be able to understand and discern what the VeriChip really is. Hallelujah!

Revelation 13:16-18

"Also it causes all, both small and great, both rich and poor, both free and slave, to be marked on the right hand or the forehead, so that no one can buy or sell unless he has the mark, that is, the name of the beast or the number of its name. This calls for wisdom: let the one who has understanding calculate the number of the beast, for it is the number of a man, and his number is 666."

Revelation 14:9-12

"And another angel, a third, followed them, saying with a loud voice, 'If anyone worships the beast and its image and receives a mark on his forehead or on his hand, he also will drink the wine of God's wrath, poured full strength into the cup of his anger, and he will be tormented with fire and sulfur in the presence of the holy angels and in the presence of the Lamb. And the smoke of their torment goes up forever and ever, and they have no rest, day or night, these worshipers of the beast and its image, and whoever receives the mark of its name.'

"Here is a call for the endurance of the saints, those who keep the commandments of God and their faith in Jesus."

VeriChip is the abbreviation for Verification Chip, and it is also called the "PositiveID" or "Biochip." This chip is implanted under the skin of your hand or forehead, and it is actually just twice the size of a small grain of rice. It is currently implanted on animals to tag pets, and it will be implanted on every human being sooner or later. However, the Lord made it clear that this is the mark of the best, 666; therefore, we should not receive it.

VeriChip could give access to the user's personal information, medical records, and even the user's genes. So in the near future, we will no longer need paper bills and those who are not chipped will not be able to purchase or sell things.

This microchip implant contains a memory that holds 16 digits of unique identification number. There are 9 digits of numbers for social security numbers in the U.S. and it is known to be enough to create distinct social security numbers for the whole American population, which is estimated to be about 300 million. However, the combinations of 16 digit numbers would be enough to create different identification number for the entire population of this world, which surpasses 6.5

billion. Therefore, this supports the anti-Christ to rule over the whole world. And this chip will also hold 128 different codes of the user's genes, so the time will come when all human beings will be controlled through technology. The charging of this device will also be done through the human body temperature; which is exactly why it is going to be implanted under the forehead or the hand, since these are the parts that are mostly prone to temperature changes.

Please see the link below if you are interested about knowing more about VeriChip.

http://blog.naver.com/PostView.nhn?blogId=sostv114&logNo=140160083793

http://www.ridingthebeast.com/articles/verichip-implant/

Images:

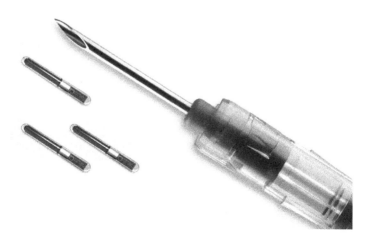

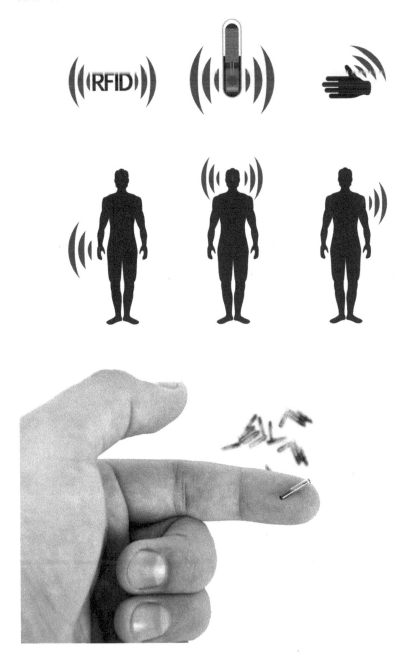

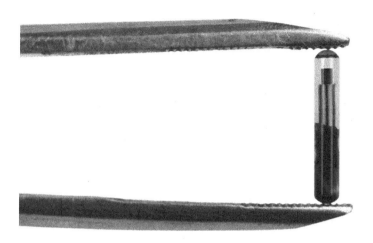

These are the images of the VeriChip implant that is injected under the skin.

Lithium batteries are used in VeriChips; thus the device is extremely flammable. As a matter of fact, it is known to be capable of exploding under water once it is flamed. (There are various side effects caused by lithium batteries and one of them is the formation of tumors. There have been reports about tumors being formed in mouse and other pet animals after lithium battery had been implanted on them).

Revelation 16:2
"So the first angel went and poured out his bowl on the earth, and harmful and painful sores came upon the people who bore the mark of the beast and worshiped its image."

Revelation 20:4-6

"Then I saw thrones, and seated on them were those to whom the authority to judge was committed. Also I saw the souls of those who had been beheaded for the testimony of Jesus and for the word of God, and those who had not worshiped the beast or its image and had not received its mark on their foreheads or their hands. They came to life and reigned with Christ for a thousand years. The rest of the dead did not come to life until the thousand years were ended. This is the first resurrection. Blessed and holy is the one who shares in the first resurrection! Over such the second death has no power, but they will be priests of God and of Christ, and they will reign with him for a thousand years."

Therefore, we should never receive the microchip. I don't know if it will be exposed to us by the name of VeriChip or PositiveID. Everybody will be forced to be chipped for three and a half years after the anti-Christ has begun its work. We should be able to endure those times. The moment this microchip will be implanted under our skin, the Holy Spirit will leave us and we will be headed to eternal life in the furious fire.

The Lord specifically commanded me, **"Tell the people NOT to receive it."**

The next place where the Lord took me was to a room that was surrounded by golden walls, with a golden floor and a golden table.

Where am I? I was very curious. Then I noticed the Apostle Paul coming towards me from one corner. *Oh yeah! The Lord had left me in this very room yesterday and the Apostle Paul was there too!* Although I was placed in that room the day before, I was not able to stay for long because I had to go down to earth. That may be the reason why the Lord brought me to this place again today.

As the Lord was about to leave me with the Apostle Paul, He knew I was a bit afraid so He said, "I won't go anywhere" and sat by the table. Then, Paul spread out a large map of the world on the table. In an instant, a gray line was drawn on the map indicating the places he had went during his first, second, and third mission journeys.

And I sensed that Paul and Jesus were pondering where I should go. I have always thought that if I had to go abroad for missions, it would be limited to just one single country. But the Lord revealed to my heart that that will not be the case, that I will be going to various places.

The Apostle Paul had gone from place to place, staying in one area for about six months and the next area for about a year and a half and so on. That was the reason why the Lord allowed me to meet Paul. He wanted to show me where Paul had gone for missions through the map. *I see... I am not called to be a missionary in one single place but in various places. Hallelujah!*

The next thing I realized was that all of the Apostle Paul's spiritual gifts would be imparted on me as well. It was revealed to my heart that I too would be able to heal the sick and even raise the dead just as Paul had. I then took off my crown and placed my head against the table. Paul then laid his hands over my head, and the Lord also laid His hand over and prayed over me. They prayed that all of the spiritual gifts and power would dwell in me and that miracles will happen when I proclaim words of faith. Hallelujah!

I then returned to the gates of Heaven and came back on earth through the carriage.

Acts 20:7-12

"On the first day of the week, when we were gathered together to break bread, Paul talked with them, intending to depart on the next day, and he prolonged his speech until midnight. There were many lamps in the upper room where we were gathered. And a young man named Eutychus, sitting at the window, sank into a deep sleep as Paul talked still longer. And being overcome by sleep, he fell down from the third story and was taken up dead. But Paul went down and bent over him, and taking him in his arms, said, 'Do not be alarmed, for his life is in him.' And when Paul had gone up and had broken bread and eaten, he conversed with them a long while, until daybreak, and so departed. And they took the youth away alive, and were not a little comforted."

26

Say "I did it through God's resources" instead of "God has done it"

(11/26/13)

The Lord and I took a walk in the beautiful garden full of fresh flowers. We found a side road so we continued walking. As we were still walking, a cloud approached us. As I hopped onto the cloud, it took me to the History Museum of the Creation of Mankind. However, I was by myself because the Lord had not ridden with me. Entering the museum on my own, one person turned around to greet me.

I was by myself in the museum, which meant that I was free to go around wherever I wanted and see whatever I wanted. I have always been so curious about the end times, so I rushed to the second floor above. I finally arrived at the second floor and it was where the seven seals, seven trumpets, seven bowls and plagues were displayed. I could see the riders of the three horses from the first, second, and third seal. But I could barely see where the sixth and seventh seal were. The Lord has not permitted yet to reveal this to me. Maybe that was why He didn't come with me today. I couldn't see it, so I went back downstairs.

And the Lord came. We both headed to my house. I noticed He was carrying the map of the world. When I asked Him about Pastor OOO, I could tell that He didn't want to talk about him anymore. But I insisted and asked, "Lord, what should I do so that I won't end up like Pastor OOO?" The Lord said, "Just fix your eyes on me, and don't lose your focus. Remember this. You people are my servants. I am the one who do the work. I am the one in charge in expanding the Kingdom of God, in saving souls, and everything else. So when people thank you and praise your work, say '**The Lord was the One who did this.**' And even when you do good deeds through your own personal money say, '**I did it through the Lord's resources**' for everything in this world is mine. And give thanks for everything for everything is done through me. Give thanks for what I have done."

Then I returned to earth. That's right, even when we give away something of our own, nothing is ours, but it is all of the Lord. We are merely to be faithful and good stewards of His resources. Hallelujah! Praise the Lord.

Psalm 24:1

"The earth is the LORD's and the fullness thereof, the world and those who dwell therein."

Haggai 2:8

"The silver is mine, and the gold is mine, declares the LORD of hosts."

Luke 3:16

"John answered them all, saying, 'I baptize you with water, but he who is mightier than I is coming, the strap of whose sandals I am not worthy to untie. He will baptize you with the Holy Spirit and fire.'"

1 Thessalonians 5:18

"Give thanks in all circumstances; for this is the will of God in Christ Jesus for you."

27

The aborted children in Heaven

(11/27/13)

Last night, I asked the Lord several times to enable me to see Heaven, but it didn't happen. After taking a moment to reflect why this must be so, I was reminded of the argument I had with my mother the day before. I realized this was the reason why I could not see Heaven – I had not fully repented.

So I prayed in the morning before God to forgive me and repented for my sins. Then I went to my mother and asked for her forgiveness, then prayed again for about an hour and a half and was brought to Heaven.

The angel who came to pick me up said, "Come, master. The Lord is waiting for you" and took me to Heaven. The Lord was dressed in a long, white gown and was draped around with a purple mantle. He warmly greeted me, and we both got on the clear, white clouds that came before us.

The Lord took me to a pond-like place. At the edge of the pond were about ten or more ladies dressed in white garments. All of them were facing towards the pond with their hands tightly holding together. Interestingly, there were naked fetuses floating on the pond against their backs. All of these fetuses had their eyes closed. And as I took a closer look at the pond, I realized that it was actually blood not water.

When the parents of the babies repent of their sins, a clear bright light comes down on the baby, and the ladies at the edge of the pond place their entire attention on that particular baby. They put their hands together and pray wholeheartedly, "Please. We pray that this child will be saved…"

If the Lord accepts the repentance prayer of the parents, the baby angels with wings will take the baby out from the pond and hand it to the ladies standing by. Then the ladies will take the baby to a public bathing room where the babies are bathed. The bathing room looked extremely beautiful. It had a very large bathtub and smaller ones right beside it for cold and hot tubs.

The size of the bathtub where the little ones were bathed was as little as the cold and hot tubs. The tub color was green and the water inside it was really clear and clean. The edges of the floors of the tub were decorated with diamonds.

At that moment, I felt how much the Lord ached for the little ones who have been abandoned. I felt like His pain for them was similar to the pain He had gone through when He was crowned with the crown of thorns on earth.

And just when I was asking myself who the ladies by the pond were, it was revealed to my heart that they were the ones who had come to Heaven first, and that each of them was given different tasks in Heaven. It was also revealed to me that these ladies had volunteered to do the task. A while later, a woman dressed in green, with a white cloth wrapped around her head, came. She was the one in charge of overseeing all the work there. She had come to check whether the ladies were doing their work properly.

Then the Lord took me through the clouds to another place. I don't recall getting off the cloud, but before I was even aware, I saw the Lord opening a glass door and entering it. There was another glass door inside, and a glass box inside. Inside the glass box were two golden stone tablets. The Ten Commandments that God had given to Moses in Mount Sinai were printed on these two golden tablets.

I was suddenly reminded by the fact that when the first Roman Catholic Pope was appointed around 600 AD, the Pope had deleted the second commandment, which states "You shall not make for yourself a carved image, or any likeness of anything that is in heaven above, or that is in the earth beneath, or that is in the water under the earth," and replaced it with a part of the 10th commandment which is "You shall not covet your neighbor's house. You shall not covet your neighbor's wife, or his male or female servant, his ox or donkey, or anything that belongs to your neighbor." In other words, the Pope had divided the tenth commandment into two separate commandments and got rid of the actual second commandment. So I tried to ask the Lord about this, but even before I opened my mouth, the Lord already knew my thoughts. I could strongly sense His great wrath.

And then, the very man who had changed the order of the Ten Commandments suddenly was seen before my eyes. He was being severely tormented in Hell. Similar to the baking pans with potholes, there was large pan with holes where the man was placed in one of the holes. He was crammed inside so he couldn't move properly, and one of the devil's minions kept on striking his head by the end of the spear. *Could it be because he had used his brain to come up with the evil idea to divide the tenth commandment into two commandments in order to make people legitimately worship the idol of Mary?* I was not sure.

Then the devil's minion flipped the iron pan upside down over the blazing fire. The man did not fall from the iron pan but was still being tortured by the fire.

In one corner, I noticed the idols of Buddha lay there. The devil's minions who were tormenting them far exceeded the number of minions who were torturing other people in Hell. They looked like robots and were very sturdy and strong. Their eyes all looked the same as well. It may be because they were dealing with the leading figures who had led numerous people astray.

After I saw the idol of Buddha, an old man suddenly came to sight. He didn't have any hair because they had been burnt from the fire. He said, "If only I knew I would end up like this..." and then began to curse.

Before I knew, I was back inside the glass house. Then I asked the Lord, "Lord, can Catholic people be saved too?" The Lord replied, "Even among the Catholics, those who have been redeemed by my blood and those who serve me with a sincere heart are saved. But those who identify me with Mary will not receive salvation." *O Lord...*

Afterwards, I saw the house of my mother for a short while.

Deuteronomy 5:1-6

"And Moses summoned all Israel and said to them, 'Hear, O Israel, the statutes and the rules that I speak in your hearing today, and you shall learn them and be careful to do them. The LORD our God made a covenant with us in Horeb. Not with our fathers did the LORD make this covenant, but with us, who are all of us here alive today. The LORD spoke with you face to face at the mountain, out of the midst of the fire, while I stood between the LORD and you at that time, to declare to you the word of the LORD. For you were afraid because of the fire, and you did not go up into the mountain. He said: 'I am the LORD your God, who brought you out of the land of Egypt, out of the house of slavery.

Deuteronomy 5:7-21

"'You shall have no other gods before me.

"'You shall not make for yourself a carved image, or any likeness of anything that is in heaven above, or that is on the earth beneath, or that is in the water under the earth. You shall not bow down to them or serve them; for I the LORD your God am a jealous God, visiting the iniquity of the fathers on the children to the third and fourth generation of those who hate me, but showing steadfast love to thousands of those who love me and keep my commandments.

"'You shall not take the name of the LORD your God in vain, for the LORD will not hold him guiltless who takes his name in vain.

"'Observe the Sabbath day, to keep it holy, as the LORD your God commanded you. Six days you shall labor and do all your work, but the seventh day is a Sabbath to the LORD your

Sarah Seoh

God. On it you shall not do any work, you or your son or your daughter or your male servant or your female servant, or your ox or your donkey or any of your livestock, or the sojourner who is within your gates, that your male servant and your female servant may rest as well as you. You shall remember that you were a slave in the land of Egypt, and the LORD your God brought you out from there with a mighty hand and an outstretched arm. Therefore the LORD your God commanded you to keep the Sabbath day.

"'Honor your father and your mother, as the LORD your God commanded you, that your days may be long, and that it may go well with you in the land that the LORD your God is giving you.

"'You shall not murder.

"'And you shall not commit adultery.

"'And you shall not steal.

"'And you shall not bear false witness against your neighbor.

"'And you shall not covet your neighbor's wife. And you shall not desire your neighbor's house, his field, or his male servant, or his female servant, his ox, or his donkey, or anything that is your neighbor's.'"

	The Biblical 10 Commandments	The 10 Commandments of Roman Catholics
First Commandment	You shall have no other gods before me (Deuteronomy 5:7)	You shall not have other gods besides me
Second Commandment	You shall not make for yourself a carved image (Deuteronomy 5:8)	You shall not take the Name of the lord your God in vain
Third Commandment	You shall not take the name of the Lord your God in vain (Deuteronomy 5:11)	Remember to keep holy the Lord's day
Fourth Commandment	Observe the Sabbath day, to keep it holy (Deuteronomy 5:12)	Honor your father and your mother
Fifth Commandment	Honor your father and your mother (Deuteronomy 5:16)	You shall not murder
Sixth Commandment	You shall not murder (Deuteronomy 5:17)	You shall not commit adultery
Seventh Commandment	You shall not commit adultery (Deuteronomy 5:18)	You shall not steal
Eighth Commandment	You shall not steal (Deuteronomy 5:19)	You shall not bear false witness against your neighbor

Ninth Commandment	You shall not bear false witness against your neighbor (Deuteronomy 5:20)	You shall not covet your neighbor's wife
Tenth Commandment	You shall not covet your neighbor's wife. And you shall not desire anything that is your neighbor's (Deuteronomy 5:21)	You shall not covet your neighbor's goods

28

Encounter with the Apostle John
(11/28/13)

I got on the golden flower carriage that the angels had brought and went up to Heaven. The moment I met the Lord, I noticed something different. He was wearing a golden crown and a golden belt around his waist for the first time. Then I realized that I was wearing exactly the same as the Lord. I, too, was wearing a white gown with a golden belt and a golden crown.

I wasn't sure why this was so, but it felt amazing. And I was filled with so much joy at seeing the Lord that I cuddled up in His arms. Oh how I wished the time could just stop at that moment!

Then when I looked around, to my utter surprise, there were multitudes of angelic figures who were dressed in white. They were all standing and clapping their hands while facing me, and they were all saying, "Welcome, Sarah. Have a great time." I could understand what they were saying through my mind because in Heaven, you can communicate without words.

Among the crowd, there was one particular woman whom I was able to see very distinctly among others. She had a bobbed hair and her face looked like she was a very good-natured person. She was trying to stick her face out among the crowds, and I felt like she was extremely very happy to see me and welcome me. I didn't understand why she stood out to me among all the people, but I realized that that these were not angels but actually people dressed in white.

The Lord and I went for a walk along the road and the more we walked, the number of these people dressed in white decreased until all of them were gone from our sight. I could no longer see any of them; but there before us was a curved road. The twisting road was very interestingly designed, but we walked along the curves so joyfully that it was not at tiring at all. It even felt like we were sliding along the road instead of walking. Being with the Lord was pure joy to me. After walking for quite a long time, we finally saw a radiant castle from a distance. Right before the castle, the road split into two, and a picnic table was placed at the crossroads. On the further side of the crossroads, we could see a mansion that looked like a castle – it was the Apostle John's house.

Just in time, John came out to greet us. He was a young man with clear eyes and white hair with streaks of blonde that glowed.

The three of us sat around a table. The Lord sat at the far side of the table, while the Apostle John and I sat next to each other in the opposite side. Then the Lord told John to give me a pen and a paper, telling me to write down the questions I had for John. The Lord certainly knows everything that is in my mind. Although I didn't have all the questions ready beforehand, the Lord knew I would have a lot of questions for the Apostle John if I were to meet him. So I was very moved by the Lord's omnipotence once again.

John then handed me a paper and a pencil with a gentle smile and gathered his hands in anticipation for my questions. To be candid, I wanted to go directly to the topic of the end times and throw him some questions about that because that was my prime interest at heart. However, I knew that wouldn't be right so I tried my best to be patient and start off with different questions. But I felt like Jesus and John already knew what was in my heart and were proud of my self-control.

Questions:

1. My first question to the Apostle John was: "How much did you love Jesus when you were on earth?" I was so impressed with myself after asking this question.

John replied, "I loved the Lord with all my soul, my heart, my strength, and my mind."

When I heard his answer, my heart melted. And I cried out in my heart, *Lord, please help me to love You in the same way.*

Matthew 22:37-38

"And he said to him, 'You shall love the Lord your God with all your heart and with all your soul and with all your mind. This is the great and first commandment.'"

2. In the Book of John, the Apostle talks about the divine nature of Jesus and proclaimed that Jesus was God. So I asked him, **"Apostle John, how did you know that Jesus was really God?"**

At that moment, the Lord suddenly reminded me of the time when He had revealed Himself to me in a very personal way. The experience goes back to 18 years ago. It was even before I knew about the Trinity. I didn't know such a word even existed. It happened in my living room, where I used to hang a picture frame of Jesus on the wall. I used to carry this picture whenever I moved since 1990. This picture of Jesus was something that was very common at the time.

A strong, bright and lucid light suddenly twinkled from the picture and all of a sudden, I was just convicted that Jesus is Lord. The light wasn't flashed by somebody else; it solely came from the picture itself. It was surely God's supernatural work. At the time, nobody had taught me that Jesus is Lord, and I do not even recall hearing such a thing. But the moment I saw the lights sparkle from the picture of Jesus, it just made sense to me to believe that Jesus is the true God. Hallelujah!

It was entirely the grace of God. Just like that, I have come to believe that Jesus is Lord through a divine revelation. God's divine intervention led me from utter disbelief to absolute faith in Him. This incident made me realize that in the same way, Apostle John also came to believe that Jesus is God through God's divine revelation to him. Hallelujah!

That was why he could boldly proclaim that the Word was God (John 1:1) and that the Word became Flesh. The Lord reminded me of my personal experience to make me understand that John came to know the Truth through God's divine revelation as well. Amen.

This is right. We humans do not have the ability to believe or know God without His divine intervention. Therefore, it is God who does 99% of the work in order for a lost soul to become saved and get to know God in a deeper way. No matter how much we work for our salvation, we cannot exceed 1% of God's redemptive work for our lives. Thus, how foolish are we to be boasting about our righteousness and how much we have done? How prone are we to give the glory to ourselves, instead of returning it to God who had made known to us through grace and divine revelation?

John 1:1

"In the beginning was the Word, and the Word was with God, and the Word was God."

John 1:14

"And the Word became flesh and dwelt among us, and we have seen his glory, glory as of the only Son from the Father, full of grace and truth."

3. My third question for John was about how he felt when he was sent to the island called Patmos for testifying about Jesus and the Word of God. He told me that because he had gone to Patmos meditating about the crucifixion of Jesus, the trials he had went through were nothing compared to what Jesus had gone through. Amen.

4. I asked my fourth question to the Lord. I asked Him why He had chosen to reveal about the end times to Apostle John. Out of all the people, I was curious why it had to be John.

And the Lord said, "I had intentionally sent John to Patmos to reveal to him about the end times." Hallelujah. I knew there were more underlying truths in this answer. I understood that it is during the times of trials and persecutions that we encounter the Lord in a more intimate way, and that the Lord had to take John to such a remote, solitary place so that he could encounter God more deeply and so that God could reveal Himself to John in a wider scale. Amen. Hallelujah.

Revelation 1:9-11

"I, John, your brother and partner in the tribulation and the kingdom and the patient endurance that are in Jesus, was on the island called Patmos on account of the word of God and the testimony of Jesus. I was in the Spirit on the Lord's Day, and I heard behind me a loud voice like a trumpet saying, 'Write what you see in a book and send it to the seven churches, to Ephesus and to Smyrna and to Pergamum and to Thyatira and to Sardis and to Philadelphia and to Laodicea.'"

5. I asked my fifth question to the Lord. I asked Him why He had asked John to take care of his mother, Mary, before He died on the cross. After I asked Him this question, He revealed the answer to me through my mind. He said that it was because His brothers at the time did not believe in Him. He didn't say anything further.

6. Again, I asked my sixth question to the Lord: "Lord, are there currently any antichrists and false prophets in the world?" He

said that they are still working under the table and have not risen to the surface yet.

7. I asked the Lord why He will come to cast the anti-Christ and the false prophets to the lake of fire. And the Lord said that it was to quickly enter into the Millennium.

8. I asked the Lord, "When will the Rapture take place?" And the Lord cited Revelation 3:10, saying, **"Because you have kept my word about patient endurance, I will keep you from the hour of trial that is coming on the whole world, to try those who dwell on the earth."** He said that He will lift those He loves into the air before the Great Tribulation. Those who couldn't go up have to pass the tribulation, and among those people, there will also be souls that will be purified through the tribulations.

9. My next question was, "Then around when will Rapture take place?" And the Lord said, "I am now standing at the door." Thus, once He opens the door, it will start taking place.

10. I asked Him further, "Lord, who will be taken in the Rapture then?" And the Lord said, "Those who are willing to become one with me." I asked, "Not those who are already united with You?" He replied, "No, those who are willing to become one with me. There is nobody in the world who has become perfectly united with me already."

The Lord knows our weaknesses and shortcomings very well. Thus, He said that those who strive to live a holy life spiritually and physically will be taken in the Rapture. I asked, "Those who strive to be holy spiritually and physically?" He said, "Yes. With my help, that is."

I started having more questions in my mind. I couldn't stop thinking where I would stand, whether I was trying hard enough to become united with the Lord, whether I would be qualified to be taken in the Rapture. (Now that I look back, I am sure that the Lord and John knew what was going through my mind at the time because everything in my heart and mind are transparent in Heaven.)

11. My next question was, "Lord, what is the message I ought to preach in this generation? How should I preach it to the people?"

And the Lord said, "Haven't I told you? I am the One who was and the One who still is and the One who is coming soon."

"Lord, since the prophecies that are not yet fulfilled are about the One who is coming, then I guess I should preach about that?"

"That is right. Tell the people to ready themselves for my coming. That means they have to purify their souls, spirits,

129

and bodies. And I should be their one and only God in their hearts... there should not be anything else besides me."

12. Then the Lord said that He had some things that He wanted to discuss with the Apostle John. So He let me go, and I came down.

It was when my spirit returned to my physical body that I realized the following things:

First, the Lord was so gracious to me. The fact that the Lord and I were wearing the same outfit and the same crown for the first time was a gesture of His grace and love. While He was wearing a golden crown and a golden belt around his long white gown, I too was wearing the same crown and belt. I now realize that God has planned this to be so because He knew ahead that we would be meeting the Apostle John and would talk about the Rapture. The Lord also knew beforehand that I would ask Him who would be taken in the Rapture and whether I would be qualified to be one of them since He said that only those who are willing to become one with Him would be raptured. The Lord knew I would be questioning about these matters, so He had prepared ahead so that we would look alike when I arrived in Heaven to say implicitly that I am one of the people who is willing to become one with Him. I am very grateful....

But I feel very ashamed when I think about whether I could be taken in the Rapture or not. I strongly feel that I do not have the right to be raptured because I know very well how sinful I really am. It is very humbling to think that the Lord has regarded me as one of the people who desire to be one with Him. *Do I really deserve such love?* I really wanted to cry. It is terrifying to think how my life would have looked like if it weren't for the cross of Jesus.

Secondly, I realized that the multitudes of people that I saw in Heaven who were dressed in white were the multitudes of people written in the Book of Revelation.

Thirdly, I realized the fact that God's revelations have been completed through the Bible alone. I realized that no matter how much I yearned to know more through my visits to Heaven, nothing more than what has already been written in the Bible is and will be revealed to me. Hallelujah!

I praise God for revealing these truths to me.

Revelations 22:18-19

"I warn everyone who hears the words of the prophecy of this book: if anyone adds to them, God will add to him the plagues described in this book, and if anyone takes away from the words of the book of this prophecy, God will take away his share in the tree of life and in the holy city, which are described in this book."

29

Where dictators and the people who love money end up

(11/28-29/13)

I asked the Lord to show me the dictator OOO.

Suddenly, I saw a man who was clinging to the edge of a cliff, looking towards us. Then a minion of the devil came and tied a rope around his neck and pulled the two ends of the rope so tightly that it broke the man's neck; only the head was hanging on the cliff. I could see the remaining bones of the neck dangling down. The man's body from his neck down had already fallen down the cliff, so it was just his head that was hanging from the cliff. However, his eyes were open and he even spoke as if he were alive.

Below the cliff, there were numerous large, dark brown cobra-like creatures. These flat and nasty creatures devoured all the bodies that were dropped to them.

In a few distance from where the dictator OOO was, another dictator, OOO, came into sight. The second dictator's body from his neck down had also fallen down the cliff, and he too was speaking with just his head hanging down the cliff. The two were cursing at each other. The cobra-like snakes had also gobbled up the body of the second dictator. Strangely, their bodies appeared again and re-attached to their necks, then their necks were broken from the tight ropes again and the snakes devoured their bodies again.

Luke 16:20-26

"And at his gate was laid a poor man named Lazarus, covered with sores, who desired to be fed with what fell from the rich man's table. Moreover, even the dogs came and licked his sores. The poor man died and was carried by the angels to Abraham's side. The rich man also died and was buried, and in Hades, being in torment, he lifted up his eyes and saw Abraham far off and Lazarus at his side. And he called out, 'Father Abraham, have mercy on me, and send Lazarus to dip the end of his finger in water and cool my tongue, for I am in anguish in this flame.' But Abraham said, 'Child, remember that you in your lifetime received your good things, and Lazarus in like manner bad things; but now he is comforted here, and you are in anguish. And besides all this, between us and you a great chasm has been fixed, in order that those who would pass from here to you may not be able, and none may cross from there to us.'"

Then I saw the people who were very greedy for money, in Hell. Whenever the devil's minions tried to fill the place with paper money, the spirits buried themselves in the money. The paper bills then turned into a mud puddle, where the people began to submerge and painfully sink into a swamp made of money.

I saw a woman, who had also loved money, in great affliction. There was a rack that had images of money. The moment the naked woman cried out, "Money!" and touched the paper bills, she was thrown to the racks where her body would be nailed to the pointed nails that were sticking out. There were four different divisions in each rack and such racks were laid out everywhere. Each of the devil's minions threw the woman around the different racks; and every time she was thrown into the rack, she would get badly hurt by the long, pointed nails. I could see her bleeding all over, and she was in deep pain and agony.

Deuteronomy 5:7
"You shall have no other gods before me."

Matthew 6:24

"No one can serve two masters, for either he will hate the one and love the other, or he will be devoted to the one and despise the other. You cannot serve God and money."

30

Where the alcoholics end up

(12/2/13)

As soon as I arrived in Heaven, the Lord allowed about six soldiers to escort me to Hell. These armed angels were in silver armor suits and were fully armed with weapons. The Lord bid me to have a safe trip, and along with the armed angels, I went down to a deep tunnel that never seemed to have an end. It was so pitch black inside the tunnel that none of us could even see each other's faces. Then there we were, at the entrance of Hell.

I could already feel the burning heat as we approached nearer to Hell.

After we came out of the tunnel, we were standing on a steep cliff where a huge fire pit was underneath us. The armed soldiers stood in line to protect me and make sure nobody could harm me. As we were standing there above the cliff, we could see in the opposite side the entrance to the tunnel that led to Hell. And there was a furious fire underneath that tunnel that was blazing to the top like a violent wind. I recognized this place because the Lord had shown it me and explained that it was where the nonbelievers end up. So I wanted to see a different place this time. Then I suddenly found myself exiting to a different tunnel with the armed angels. We arrived in a place where I had taken a short glimpse of a few days ago. In that place, there was a pit that was deeply caved in, and two figures whose heads were all white were coming out from the pit. I was confused because I couldn't understand how such people with pure white head could come out from Hell. It was strange to me, but when I tried not to look, I could no longer see them again.

In both Heaven and Hell, I noticed that there are many times if I try not to see something, it will no longer be seen. This happened most of the time, except when the Lord really wanted me to see something against my will. I could no longer see the two figures with white heads, but I couldn't stop wondering what that must have been. It certainly looked like they were humans who were crawling out of the pit, but I couldn't understand what I saw. *Why were their entire face and hair white?*

Besides their eyes, everything was white and looked ask if their heads were covered with white cloths. Before I knew it, I was in that place again where I had seen them. I finally got the answer to my questions.

As I looked closely into the pit, I realized that it was actually white maggots, hundreds of thousands of them, which had covered their faces and hairs. The pit was filled with swarms of maggots. I was curious what kind of people end up getting this punishment for eternity, and it was revealed to me right away that these were the people who had been addicted to alcohol during their lifetime in the world. They were those who had sold their souls to alcohol, rather than God. *Oh Lord!*

1 Corinthians 3:16-17

"Do you not know that you are God's temple and that God's Spirit dwells in you? If anyone destroys God's temple, God will destroy him. For God's temple is holy, and you are that temple."

Then the scene shifted to a different place where people were hanging onto a very large cliff in different positions and were being tortured by the devil's minions. The cliff was extremely high and countless number of people was hanging on to the cliff, each receiving a different punishment.

No one punishment was the same; everybody was being tormented in a different way. I couldn't understand why the Lord had allowed me to see this sight of multitudes of people going through so much pain in this cliff. I could see some globally recognized dictators being tortured by the devil's minions, and even people who had destroyed their families by committing adulteries – everybody being hit until their buttocks burst. After seeing this horrendous sight, I came out.

31

Conversation with Lucifer

(12/3/13)

I went up to Heaven just like the former times; and upon arrival, I thought I saw the Light of the Lord shine for a second but then He disappeared out of sight. Not even the armed angels could be seen. I was confused for a second. Then I started feeling contractions around my neck and began to panic. *Why am I feeling this pain when I am in Heaven? What's happening to my body? Why am I feeling crippled?*

It was later that I found out that the reason I went through this was because of Lucifer. I was feeling disabled because of the influence of Satan. In other words, it was a sign that boded the coming of Lucifer.

I cannot think of a better explanation because right after experience such discomfort, Lucifer suddenly appeared before my eyes.

A tremendously large face that covered my whole range of vision appeared. The entire face was green, and its eyes and head were shaped like an owl. I was so shocked and thought, *Who can this be?* But right at that moment, I knew who it was. It was Lucifer, the deceiver of the whole world.

Then a scenario flashed through my head. It was the scene of the Freemasons making ceremonial rituals before a figure of an owl. It clicked to me that they are actually worshiping Lucifer. I couldn't believe Lucifer was right in front of me. It was a little bit frightening.

So I whispered in my mind, "Lord." Although I couldn't see the Lord, I felt Him whispering in my ears right behind me, saying, "Listen to what he has to say."

Then Lucifer spoke up: "Hahahahahahaha! I am indeed deceiving the whole world! Hahahahaha!" The sound of his laughter was extremely irritating and piercing.

I then said, "But there are the people of God" and flatly asked, "Who is the antichrist?"

He then cited the Word of God and said, "Hahahahaha! It's the one who sits at the Temple of God and claims that he is God!"

I asked again, "Who is he?"

"Hahahahaha! You really want to know? He will appear soon."

I was thinking in my mind that in order for that antichrist to sit at the Temple of God, the Temple should be built first. But Lucifer knew what I was thinking and said, "That work has already been begun." This Temple refers to the Third Temple that the Jewish people are trying to construct.

I asked Lucifer, "You know about VeriChip, right?"

Then Lucifer said, "The whole world will come under my thumb through VeriChip. Hahahahahaha!"

Oh my goodness! So I asked again, "Who are the false prophets?"

And he replied, "They too are my servants. Hahahahahahahaha! I am actually spreading homosexuality all over the world. Hahahaha! By experiencing the height of pleasure in their peripheral nerves, they will reject God. Hahahaha!"

His words made me so furious that I said, "But you know that you don't have much time left, right?"

And he said, "I know. But I am working my best to degenerate the lives of people and lead them to the eternal lake of fire. Hahahahaha!"

I suddenly became so afraid, so I whispered in my mind "Lord" for the second time. And again, the Lord whispered to my ears, "Listen to what he has to say."

Then I became astute. I asked, "What kind of people do you hate most?"

"I absolutely abhor those who read the Word of God and pray! No matter how much I try to tempt them, they just would not give in to me!"

"What disgusts you most?"

Suddenly, there was a quiver in his voice. In a shaky voice he said, "The blood of Jesus. We become powerless just by hearing those words. All of our plans falter and our efforts crumble to dust."

As I was listening to him, I realized how vital it is to proclaim the Blood of Jesus over my life continuously and to cover my loved ones with the Blood of Jesus every single day.

"What about the Name of Jesus?"

"That too! Whenever we hear that, we can't do anything but retreat. All of our plans get destroyed whenever one uses the name of Jesus."

Something quickly came into my mind. *Aha! Then that means I can cancel everything that is bad in Jesus' Name.... I can cancel all the curses I have spit out of my mouth in Jesus' Name...*

I asked him again, "What kind of people can you not attack?"

"Those who give praises to God, serve, love, live in harmony, and sacrifice. I cannot do anything to them."

"Then when can you work actively?"

"When people are jealous and envy one another.... That's the easiest time for us to work. We just dive into their lives."

The Lord was the One who had allowed me to have a conversation with Lucifer. It was something totally unplanned and unexpected. Hallelujah. Praise God.

Revelation 12:9
"And the great dragon was thrown down, that ancient serpent, who is called the devil and Satan, the deceiver of the whole world—he was thrown down to the earth, and his angels were thrown down with him."

Isaiah 14:12-15

"How you are fallen from heaven,

O Day Star, son of Dawn!

How you are cut down to the ground,

you who laid the nations low!

You said in your heart,

'I will ascend to heaven;

above the stars of God

I will set my throne on high;

I will sit on the mount of assembly

in the far reaches of the north;

I will ascend above the heights of the clouds;

I will make myself like the Most High.'

But you are brought down to Sheol,

to the far reaches of the pit."

Genesis 3:1-4

"Now the serpent was more crafty than any other beast of the field that the LORD God had made. He said to the woman, 'Did God actually say, "You shall not eat of any tree in the garden?"' And the woman said to the serpent, 'We may eat of the fruit of the trees in the garden, but God said, "You shall not eat of the fruit of the tree that is in the midst of the garden, neither shall you touch it, lest you die."' But the serpent said to the woman, 'You will not surely die.'"

32

Where stubborn Christians end up
(12/5/13)

There have always been two angels who come to pick me up on a golden, floral carriage. One of them would be in charge of the horse, while the other angel would always be standing outside the carriage to greet me. Both of these angels have no wings and are dressed in white gowns that look like the ones the priests used to wear in an older era.

The angel who was attending me outside said, "Welcome, master. Please get in." *Wow, this angel just called me 'master.'*

I got on the carriage and realized that it had been a little over a day since I'd last seen the Lord. I missed Him so much and couldn't wait to see Him again.

As the carriage arrived in Heaven, Jesus was standing on my right side to greet me, as He always did. He said, "Welcome, my daughter, my bride." As soon as I saw the Lord, I threw myself to the hem of His gown because I had missed Him so much.

Strangely, there was a woman who was standing to my left, welcoming me. She was wearing a beautiful golden crown and there was a big precious stone right at the center of her crown. I had no idea who this gorgeous woman was. As I was thinking this, I suddenly found myself flying on the clouds with the Lord, with the woman left behind.

(I later found out that the woman was Mary, who had given birth to Jesus. I don't know why but her identity was kept from me that day). The speed of the clouds today was extremely fast, much faster than at ordinary times.

I almost felt like we were riding an airplane; I somehow knew the Lord was taking me to a far, faraway place. We flew over the mountains at a full speed. I was so curious where He was taking me.

Then suddenly, all of the beauty and wonders of Heaven disappeared out of sight; instead, a heavy feeling of desolation filled in and I began to feel my whole body being sucked into something. The next thing I saw was a pale, feeble spirit that had fallen flat on the ground. The body looked very flabby and mushy, as if it didn't have any bones. It also looked so weak like one who has been

malnourished. I became so afraid that I was about to turn and call on the Lord, but thankfully He was right there, beside me.

While this spirit was lying flat on the ground, there was another spirit right in the next cell. There were no iron bars, no devil's minions around, no serpents, and no tools for torturing in this place. But the place was divided into rooms with just a single wall in between; thus it was hard to see where the dividing mark between the two rooms was.

The spirit that was in the next cell suddenly spoke to me, in English, "I loved God. But I am here. I never tried to keep His commandments. I always lived my own way."

He was explaining to me why he was there. The spirit also said that he had attended church, but he had ignored God's commandments and lived according to the desires of his flesh. That's why he ended up coming here after he died. *Oh Lord!*

As I was listening to him, I thought to myself, *Where is this place?* And before I knew it, I fell into deep sleep. But even after I woke up, I didn't stop wondering where that could have been. I certainly remember seeing a place that was quite similar to this one.

33

The Lord's Private Room

(12/6/13)

I went up to Heaven. Once again, the Lord and the beautiful woman were waiting for me to greet me. Just like the day before, the Lord was standing on my right side, while the woman was on my left. I noticed that the Lord was standing very close to me, while the woman was a bit more distant from where I was. Strangely, it just dawned on me supernaturally that this woman was Mary so told the Lord, "Lord, she is Mary!" and He replied, "You're right."

He continued, "Let's go to my private room." *Wow! To the Lord's private room!* I couldn't contain my excitement like a little kid. I was so excited that the shoulders of my physical body on earth were moving up and down. It is very strange but whenever I get so thrilled in Heaven, my physical body on earth responds as well.

Before I knew it, the Lord and I had already entered in His room, and we were sitting down. The three of us, the Lord, Mary, and I, sat around a luxurious round table. The Lord was holding some papers and asked me if I wanted to listen to his music. Those papers were filled with musical notes.

As soon as I said yes, a choir that was composed of baby angels suddenly appeared from our right side. The conductor of the choir was an angel too, and looked older than the choir members. All of them had wings, and as the music played, they began to sing "Jingle Bells, Jingle Bells."

It was very surreal to hear the song Jingle Bells in Heaven!

I was so happy because I felt like it was a gift from the Lord since Christmas was near. It suddenly dawned on me why Mary kept on showing up with the Lord. It was because the day of His birth on earth was approaching.

Then the Lord called my name, "Sarah."

"Yes," I answered.

"What do you want to do for me?" He asked.

"I want to bring you joy," I said and Mary smiled.

The Lord then spread out the map of the world, and reminded me of what He had said and commanded me before – to go on a mission tour. He had told me to go to Mexico first, then to Africa, China, Japan, Israel, Turkey, Greece, etc., for missions and to testify about what I have seen in Heaven and Hell. Hallelujah. *Yes, Lord. I will follow.*

34

Where thieves end up

(12/6/13)

As soon as I went up to Heaven, the Lord placed four armed angels who were wearing black masks over their eyes, to accompany me to Hell. The Lord did not come with me but allowed these fully armed angels to escort me to Hell.

We arrived at the place where the thieves end up in Hell; and once we entered there, I could already sense the attack of the devil's minions whose faces looked like snakes. Right at that moment, one of the angels who accompanied me repulsed the attacks. Then I heard the sounds of swords and spears colliding against each other, and suddenly a scene of people being tormented with various punishments unfolded before my eyes.

1. The first thing that stood out to me was two or three minions which looked like aliens tormenting a naked man. There was a round, glass aquarium that was the size of a small house, which was made of two plies. The minions were jamming the man in between these two plies. The space in between was too narrow and even filled with water, so they were forcefully pushing him, causing immense pain and agony to the man. These alien-like minions were giggling and laughing at the man who was being tortured, and they went up to the top of the aquarium and started running around. I later found out that this particular man had secretly taken his father's money and used it for his own. Therefore, using one's father's property in secret is also considered as stealing.

2. The second thing that caught my attention in the same place was a man who lost one arm, being carried away by the devil's minions through a stretcher. He was heavily bleeding, and it was revealed to me supernaturally that this particular man had abducted children with his arms. So this is what happened to those who kidnapped children.

3. The next thing I saw was in the far end side of the same place. I saw a naked man who was hanging on a cross in severe pain. It was revealed to me that those who were suffering in the cross were those who had been involved with burglary throughout his lifetime. Right at that moment, I suddenly was reminded of the two thieves who were crucified on the cross beside Jesus. Such people who had committed robbery were to suffer on crosses eternally.

4. On the other side, I saw a large pulley of a well, with people tied onto the pulley, which went up and down the well. Whenever the pulley went down the well, it tortured these people. I realized that these were the people who had stolen other people's belongings.

5. To the corner of the left side, I saw several blades of a knife that were pointing up. Then the bodies of people were horizontally thrown to where these blades where standing, cutting their bodies into several pieces. What a gruesome sight it was... I couldn't help but scream, "Oh my God!" as soon as I saw the dreadful sight. I asked the Lord, "Why are these people getting this punishment?" And the Lord revealed to me the answer in my mind. These were the people who had stolen the sacred things of God and sold them for profit.

Leviticus 5:15-16

"If anyone commits a breach of faith and sins unintentionally in any of the holy things of the LORD, he shall bring to the LORD as his compensation, a ram without blemish out of the flock, valued in silver shekels, according to the shekel of the sanctuary, for a guilt offering. He shall also make restitution for what he has done amiss in the holy thing and shall add a fifth to it and give it to the priest. And the priest shall make atonement for him with the ram of the guilt offering, and he shall be forgiven."

Deuteronomy 5:19

"And you shall not steal."

35

The Lord's Comfort

(12/6/13)

Once again, I went up to Heaven. I am not sure if it was because I had previously been in Hell, but the Lord and Mary tried to comfort me when I met them. This was probably because whenever I return from Hell, I feel weak and extremely stressed. The Lord and Mary's faces were full of empathy when they greeted me, and I could feel their comfort in my heart. Then they took me to my house. It has been a while since I last came to my own house. The carps in the pond by the garden leaped up in the air crying out, "Our master is here. Our master is here."

The three of us sat around the big, rectangular dining table in my house. The whole table and its chairs were made of gold. And Mary gave me a beautiful pearl necklace as a present.

With an aching heart, I asked the Lord about my husband. I asked the Lord whether my husband would work with me for God's Kingdom until the end. The Lord said, "Isn't that why I taught you three times through the fire of the Holy Spirit before you got married?"

I asked again, "But why are he and I are so different?" Then I remembered seeing his house, which only had a few wooden posts. Then the Lord said, "If you want, I will let you live in this house together." He also gave me an implication that my husband and I will be doing God's ministries together. Hallelujah! Praise God!

Then I came back down.

Matthew 19:5-6

"'Therefore a man shall leave his father and his mother and hold fast to his wife, and the two shall become one flesh?' So they are no longer two but one flesh. What therefore God has joined together, let not man separate."

Once I returned to my earthly home, it became clear to me that the Lord had taken me to my house in Heaven so that I may ask Him what was in my heart regarding my husband. And He also took me to my house to let me know that if I desired, He would let me live with my husband in that very house in Heaven. Hallelujah.

36

Encounter with Mary, who had broken the alabaster jar before Jesus

(12/9/13)

I went up to Heaven, and as always, the Lord was standing at the same place to greet me. Only this time, He was wearing a golden gown.

And to the left side in front of me, there was a woman who came to greet me as well. She had her hair tied up in a bun. It dawned on me supernaturally that she was Martha's sister, Mary, who had broken the alabaster jar before Jesus in preparation for His funeral. While I was wondering where the three of us would go that day, we had already arrived at my house.

We all sat in the golden long, rectangular table. The Lord and Mary both sat across me; and as soon as we were all seated, I asked Mary a question: "Mary, how were you able to break that precious alabaster jar for the Lord?"

Then Mary answered, "There should be nothing that is mine when worshiping the Lord." Hallelujah. That is exactly right. Amen. When we claim to worship the Lord, we shouldn't claim anything to be ours.

Then I carefully asked the Lord, "Lord, I am planning to take some people to the prayer mountain on December 19th to hold a testimonial revival worship service about Heaven and Hell. Will you minister to us through your fire?"

The Lord said He will and all of a sudden, His eyes turned into shape of a flame. Hallelujah. I took that as the Lord's confirmation that He will work powerfully during the revival. Hallelujah! Thank You, Lord.

Matthew 26:7-13

"A woman came up to him with an alabaster flask of very expensive ointment, and she poured it on his head as he reclined at table. And when the disciples saw it, they were indignant, saying, 'Why this waste? For this could have been sold for a large sum and given to the poor.' But Jesus, aware of this, said to them, 'Why do you trouble the woman? For she has done a beautiful thing to me.

For you always have the poor with you, but you will not always have me. In pouring this ointment on my body, she has done it to prepare me for burial. Truly, I say to you, wherever this gospel is proclaimed in the whole world, what she has done will also be told in memory of her.'"

37

Another glimpse of Hell

(12/9/13)

As soon as I arrived in Heaven, I knew the Lord was going to send me to Hell because an angel with a mask on came and stood beside me. Just as an elevator, we went down nonstop. This time, the angel who was escorting me was not armed at all. Instead, the angel was wearing a very tight outfit and was following me with crossed arms. It seemed like an endless ride until we finally arrived in the lowest ground.

There were massive round rocks that were connected to the iron chains, and these heavy rocks were rolling down from above and running over a man who was standing there. *What a horrendous punishment!* It was terrible. I was wondering what kind of people end up receiving this punishment, and it dawned on me that it was those who had embezzled public funds for their own use.

Then to my right, I saw a man who was being grinded in a millstone. His skins were being crushed and started to burst. Blood was everywhere and I could even see his intestines being grinded. It was too horrific to watch. It then dawned on me that people who have committed sexually assault and murder will end up in this place.

The angel who came with me said, "The Lord has commanded to go to that opposite side." Something that was even more terrifying was happening there. I saw a pastor who had committed immoral affairs with his church member, and he was going through an unbearable punishment inside.

Deuteronomy 5:18
"And you shall not commit adultery."

38

The heresies suffering in
the burning furnace

(12/9/13)

This was my third visit to Heaven today. An angel who was wearing a gown came to me and said, "Please follow me." He then led me to a slanted tunnel that was pointing downwards.

Nowhere was the Lord to be seen, but I asked Him anyway, "Lord, where am I going?" And although I couldn't see Him, He answered me and said, "Go and see." The Lord always answers me right away even when I cannot see him.

As we were heading down, I could already see a humongous iron pot. Inside it was a great mass of people screaming on top of their lungs.

The pot was really gigantic, and around it the blazing fire was burning furiously. I asked the Lord, "Oh Lord! Who are those people?" The Lord then revealed to me that these were the people who had served heresies and were being severely tormented in a group inside the iron pot.

John 14:6

"Jesus said to him, 'I am the way, and the truth, and the life. No one comes to the Father except through me.'"

That's what happens to those who serve heresies.

39

Encounter with Peter and John
in the History Museum

(12/10/13)

I went up to Heaven, and the Lord was standing at the same place to greet me. A beautiful woman was attending too. Her long hair was tied at the back, and she was wearing an apron. Then I noticed that the road before me was carpeted with silk all the way to the far distance. I was also wearing a dress that was decorated with a golden band that looked like a ribbon and was walking on the silk carpet road with the Lord. Walking with the Lord filled me with extreme joy and delight. I felt like a bride walking down the wedding aisle with the groom.

A small, green angel who looked like a clown then appeared, running around back and forth out of sheer excitement.

The Lord and I enjoyed our walk together and once we arrived at the end of the road, we rode on the clouds and flew to the History Museum of the Creation of Mankind. It was a long ride until the rooftop of the museum finally unveiled. The roof of the museum was green and had a spiral pattern to it. The museum itself was enormously big and surrounded by a forest. We finally entered into the museum, but nobody was there.

The picture that I saw as soon as I went in was the one depicting a sinful woman washing the feet of Jesus with her tears of repentance. I had seen this drawing before, but this time I was also able to see the picture right next to it. It showed Jesus stretching His hand to save Peter, who was almost drowning in the water. As I was looking at the picture, Peter suddenly came and stood next to us.

As always, his extremely outgoing character was evident right away, as well as his cheerful and clumsy side. Peter said, "Oh man! I don't know why I have become famous for these."

He was referring to the incidents when he had denied Jesus three times and when he walked on the water then fell because of his fear of the storm. He was venting that he had become famous for "bad" things. All three of us laughed out loud over his words.

But I consoled him in my heart by saying, "But you were surely an awesome disciple of the Lord." No words needed to be uttered out of the mouth because we could communicate through our hearts.

Then the Apostle John arrived. John was a handsome young man with blonde hair. We all then discussed where we should go and finally agreed to go the floor where the drawings of the seven churches where the Lord had sent letters to were displayed. I personally think that the Lord had intentionally called John to come because He already knew we were going to go see those pictures.

We first went to where the pictures of the Church of Laodicea were located. Laodicea was the last church to which the Lord had sent a letter. There was a large picture of the Lord standing outside the door, knocking and asking to open the door.

Laodicea was a church without the presence of God. It was a church where the people practiced religion without God. I asked the Lord, "Lord, what happens when you walk by faith without God? What happens when you yourself become the master in your religious life?" All of a sudden, I felt everybody's faces freezing. Then their faces just disappeared. I could no longer see them, and I had to come back down.

Is that the answer? Not being able to come to Heaven?

Revelation 3:15-21

"I know your works: you are neither cold nor hot. Would that you were either cold or hot! So, because you are lukewarm, and neither hot nor cold, I will spit you out of my mouth. For you say, I am rich, I have prospered, and I need nothing, not realizing that you are wretched, pitiable, poor, blind, and naked. I counsel you to buy from me gold refined by fire, so that you may be rich, and white garments so that you may clothe yourself and the shame of your nakedness may not be seen, and salve to anoint your eyes, so that you may see. Those whom I love, I reprove and discipline, so be zealous and repent. Behold, I stand at the door and knock. If anyone hears my voice and opens the door, I will come in to him and eat with him, and he with me. The one who conquers, I will grant him to sit with me on my throne, as I also conquered and sat down with my Father on his throne. The one who conquers, I will grant him to sit with me on my throne."

Why did their faces freeze right when I asked that question? Is it because it means such lukewarm Christians won't be able to sit with the Lord on His throne? Or is it because I asked the Lord to show me again when He had already shown it to me?

I would like to clarify where the people like the Laodicea Church end up going. These are the people who claim to be Christians but do not follow the commands of God. Everything I have written below are based on what the Lord had revealed through Apostle John in the

Book of Revelation. (See Chapter 23: The place of repentance, and Chapter 32: Where stubborn Christians end up)

Bible Passages	Those who conquer	Those defeated
[Revelations 2:7] He who has an ear, let him hear what the Spirit says to the churches. To the one who conquers I will grant to eat of the tree of life, which is in the paradise of God.	Will be granted to eat the tree of life.	Won't be able to eat the tree of life.
[Revelations 2:11] He who has an ear, let him hear what the Spirit says to the churches. The one who conquers will not be hurt by the second death	Will not be hurt by the second death.	Will be hurt by the second death.
[Revelations 2:17] He who has an ear, let him hear what the Spirit says to the churches. To the one who conquers I will give some of the hidden manna, and I will give him a white stone, with a new name written on the stone that no one knows except the one who receives it.	Will be given some of the hidden manna, and will be given a white stone with a new name written on it.	Will not be given the hidden manna, and will not be given a white stone with a new name written on it.

[Revelations 2:26] The one who conquers and who keeps my works until the end, to him I will give authority over the nations	Will be given authority over the nations.	Will not be given authority over the nations.
[Revelations 3:5] The one who conquers will be clothed thus in white garments, and I will never blot his name out of the book of life. I will confess his name before my Father and before his angels.	Will be clothed in white garments. His name will never be blotted out of the book of life. Thus, his name will be confessed before God and His angels.	Will not be clothed in white garments. His name will be blotted out of the book of life. Thus, his name will not be confessed before God and His angels.
[Revelations 3:12] The one who conquers, I will make him a pillar in the temple of my God. Never shall he go out of it, and I will write on him the name of my God, and the name of the city of my God, the new Jerusalem, which comes down from my God out of heaven, and my own new name.	Will become a pillar in the temple of God. The name of God, and the name of the new Jerusalem, and the new name of Jesus will be written on him.	Will not become a pillar in the temple of God. The name of God, the name of the new Jerusalem, and the new name of Jesus will not be written on him.

[Revelations 3:21] The one who conquers, I will grant him to sit with me on my throne, as I also conquered and sat down with my Father on his throne.	Will be granted to sit with Jesus on His throne.	Will not be granted to sit with Jesus on His throne.
[Revelations 21:6~7] And he said to me, "It is done! I am the Alpha and the Omega, the beginning and the end. To the thirsty I will give from the spring of the water of life without payment. The one who conquers will have this heritage, and I will be his God and he will be my son."	Will be given the spring of the water of life for free. Will become a son of God.	Will not be given the spring of the water of life. Will not be able to become a son of God.

Please refer back to page 91 (the place of repentance) and to page 146 (where stubborn Christians end up). The Bible clearly teaches us about those who conquer and those who do not. So where do those who get defeated go to? Probably to the place of repentance.

It is where the spirits have fallen down and were lying flat in the ground (page 147).

It is where they were weeping through sorrow and gnashing their teeth.

It is also where they were being severely beaten (See Volume 2).

The following words are from the Lord:

Matthew 24:48-51

"But if that wicked servant says to himself, 'My master is delayed,' and begins to beat his fellow servants and eats and drinks with drunkards, the master of that servant will come on a day when he does not expect him and at an hour he does not know and will cut him in pieces and put him with the hypocrites. In that place there will be weeping and gnashing of teeth."

Matthew 22:9-13

"'Go therefore to the main roads and invite to the wedding feast as many as you find.' And those servants went out into the roads and gathered all whom they found, both bad and good. So the wedding hall was filled with guests. But when the king came in to look at the guests, he saw there a man who had no wedding garment. And he said to him, 'Friend, how did you get in here without a wedding garment?' And he was speechless. Then the king said to the attendants, 'Bind him hand and foot and cast him into the outer darkness. In that place there will be weeping and gnashing of teeth.'"

Matthew 25:28-30

"So take the talent from him and give it to him who has the ten talents. For to everyone who has will more be given, and he will have an abundance. But from the one who has not, even what he has will be taken away. And cast the worthless servant into the outer darkness. In that place there will be weeping and gnashing of teeth."

Matthew 25:10-13

"And while they were going to buy, the bridegroom came, and those who were ready went in with him to the marriage feast, and the door was shut. Afterward the other virgins came also, saying, 'Lord, lord, open to us.' But he answered, 'Truly, I say to you, I do not know you.' Watch therefore, for you know neither the day nor the hour."

It is evident from these passages that the wicked servant, the man who had no wedding garment, the man who wasn't able to increase the amount of talents that was given to him, and the five foolish virgins who ran out of oil in their lamps while waiting for the bridegroom will not able to enter the New Jerusalem where the glory of God will shine as the sun.

40

Encounter with the one who offered five loaves and two fish to Jesus

(12/12/13)

When I went up to Heaven, the Lord was wearing a white garment. I was already wearing a crown and a white dress when the angels carried me on the sedan chair. They took me to the garden, while the Lord just walked alongside me. Then the angels left after they put me down. There were so many beautiful flowers that were orange and yellow in color.

Suddenly the orange flowers began to speak. Actually, I spoke first in my mind since you don't necessarily have to speak out loud to be heard in Heaven. I had said quietly in my mind, "These past weeks have been pretty rough on me."

Then the orange flower comforted me by saying, "It's alright. Vent it all out to the Lord." The Lord and I continued to walk until we reached the end of the garden, which was the beginning of the sandy beach. A starfish then said, "Can I come with you?" and began to leap and follow us. I was so surprised to see a starfish leaping on its own. Heaven felt like a new place yet again.

Then the Lord and I got on the clouds and went to the History Museum of the Creation of Mankind. As soon as we entered the museum, I could see the picture that illustrated the miraculous incident of the five loaves of bread and two fish. In the picture, the Lord was holding a piece of bread but the same bread was sticking together, forming a long chain. It almost looked like a chain of candies. I could tell that no matter how much the bread was broken to be shared with the people, the chain never got shorter.

I said, "Lord, I want to see the kid who had offered to give his five bread and two fish. Please show him to me." As I said these words, a young man who was quite big and bulky showed up all of a sudden. He was the very kid who had given to Jesus all he had. I was curious how great his reward must have been in Heaven for giving all he had to the Lord.

We then went to his house. It was a pink house. His house wasn't as big as the houses of the spiritual forefathers, whose houses were either very large castles or ones that actually looked like a city. In this young man's house, there was a garden that had a brook with waters flowing very peacefully. We sat around the long table in the backyard and talked. I asked him, "You were a very young boy back then, but how were you able to give all that you had to the Lord just because He needed it?"

Right at that moment, I remembered what the Lord had said and I believe He had brought this specific Bible passage into my mind because that was the answer: **"Let the little children come to me and do not hinder them."** Then the following verse also came into my mind. **"For to such belongs the kingdom of heaven."**

The little boy had given all he had to the Lord out of a pure heart when he heard the Lord needed it. Other people, especially adults, may have also brought some food with them to the mountain at the time; but it was only this boy who willingly gave everything he had brought to the Lord.

Through this boy's genuine act of obedience, the Lord was able to perform the great miracle of feeding at least 5,000 people. Thus, the Lord delighted in him who cheerfully gave all that he had to the Lord. Although it wasn't much, He took it and looked up to Heaven, said a blessing and by His almighty power, miraculously fed thousands of people. Hallelujah.

The Lord revealed to me that when we do our best to give our energy, time, and finances to Him; those will be our five loaves of breads and two fish for the Lord. Whenever we give our best to the Lord, He will look up to Heaven and bless it and use it to save lost souls. Regardless of how much or how little we give, the Lord will use it to create a big miracle in the Kingdom of God. Hallelujah!

To whom? To those who give everything they have to the Lord as the boy had done. The Lord says in **Matthew 19:14, "But Jesus said, 'Let the little children come to me and do not hinder them, for to such belongs the kingdom of heaven.'"**

Hallelujah! I praise You, Lord, with my whole heart!

PART II

How I came to believe in Jesus and God's calling on my life

The next part is about how I have come to know Jesus and how God has called me to be His servant. I pray that God's grace will be with all who read this.

1 Corinthians 15:10

"But by the grace of God I am what I am, and his grace toward me was not in vain. On the contrary, I worked harder than any of them, though it was not I, but the grace of God that is with me."

1

Why I applied to Medical School

I was born in a very small city at the southern end of Korea called Samcheonpo. My father at the time was a government official in the Office of Education, so my family had to move around frequently. I spent most of my childhood years in Samcheonpo and Jinju; so I received my primary, secondary, and post-secondary education in these two places. Then I studied at the Medical College of Ewha Women's University in Seoul and graduated as the top student from the two-year pre-medical school. I also graduated as an honor student from the four-year medical school and obtained my medical license in 1986.

The reason why I applied to Medical College stemmed all the way back to when I first heard about Albert Schweitzer in an Ethics class in fourth grade. I was deeply moved by how he had devoted his life as a medical missionary in Africa, even though he had two doctoral degrees. Since then, it had become my dream to become like him.

During my university years, I had no life. I was solely committed to my studies. And in order to maintain my status as the top one or two in class, I rarely got enough sleep because of my extensive studying. While studying at Ewha University for six years, I never even attended the famous Ewha School Festival. I thought it was a waste of time.

At that time, Doosan Group, which was famous for OB beer, provided full scholarship funding to two select medical students out of the whole nation. I was one of the two lucky students, and I actually continued to receive this scholarship until my graduation.

Starting from the third year, my medical school classes were held in the Ewha University Hospital, which was located in Dongdaemoon. All students would wear white gowns, and the clinical professors would come in to the classes and lecture. It was an exciting moment for me, but before long I noticed that every professor who came to instruct us was unintentionally talking about money and profit. I started to become extremely disappointed with them.

So I began to ask my classmates one by one, why they had chosen to come to medical school. To my utter surprise, all of the students answered it was because their parents wanted them to. They also said that they applied to medical school because once they graduate from medical school, they will be able to make a lot of money and because a doctor is a well-respected profession in the society.

Nobody, not even one, had decided to come out of compassion towards dying souls. This reality hit me hard. It was very hard to accept that all of my classmates had come to medical school to make lots of money and earn respect from people. From then on, I was ashamed about becoming a doctor.

I was filled with even greater despair because of what the clinical professors were teaching in class. One professor came to class to teach about giving emergency treatments, and what the professor said really shocked me. The professor instructed us that when a patient comes to the emergency room after an accident in the middle of the night, no matter how severely injured he or she may be, even if the person may be at the brink of death, if it was obvious that that this person was not capable of affording the medical expenses, we were not to accept him or her in the hospital.

Korea at the time did not have a structured system of medical insurance, so when emergency accidents took place, the medical cost for the essential computer scans and tests were extremely expensive. However, after being publicly instructed by the professors to send back the seriously wounded or even dying patients if they don't have money, I was extremely repulsed by the reality of the medical world. So I was firmly determined to become a famous scientist rather than a doctor after graduation. Some people may ask why I did not choose to go to Africa after graduation, like Dr. Schweitzer did. It was because I was only 22 years old, and my protective biological father would have never let his naïve daughter fly to Africa by herself at such a young age.

So I decided to work my way up to become a scientist to contribute to the issues of human health instead of becoming a doctor. Thus, right after I graduated from Ewha Medical College, I pursued my master's degree in Physiology at the Medical School of Seoul National University. After I received my master's degree three years later, I continued my studies to the doctoral level in the same program at the same school. But somehow, my heart was not satisfied. I strongly felt that I had to continue my studies in America if I wanted to become a distinguished scientist, so I started studying English and then took the TOEFL and GRE tests. Eventually, I was admitted to the Medical School of Brown University for the Ph.D. program. I came to America in July 1990 and worked really hard in academics and research. As a result, I was able to attain my doctorate in Physiology in three years.

After graduating from Brown University, I was given an opportunity to do research on the physiology of human body at the University of California Los Angeles (UCLA) for four years. During my research in UCLA, I refuted a major theory that had been predominant in the field for thirty years. I conducted a molecular research that proved the mechanism that would explain how, on the cellular level, our bodies receive signs and transmit them to the brain and how the signs from the brain are transmitted to the cell in the peripheral nerves.

As a result of this, my findings have produced significant research work that will be cited by other people for 50 to 100 years from now. My thesis has also been included in textbooks in graduate schools. (Three of my doctoral dissertations were published in the Biophysical Journal, and the results of the research I had conducted in UCLA were published in *Neuron* magazine).

Clearly, my life was centered in studies as well as my own reputation. My ultimate goal was to become a renowned scientist, after all. Now that I look back, I can only say how meaningless my life was. When I first arrived in the U.S. in the 1990s, my aim was to receive the Nobel Prize for Medicine. But it didn't take long for me to realize how unlikely that was because regardless of one's actual performances. I found out that the Nobel prizes were given to people according to the national power of their home country. I knew I had a very low chance because Korea at the time was far weaker than Japan or United States. So I had lowered my goal and changed it to having my name written in school textbooks, and it was finally achieved after I disproved the 30-year-old, leading theoretical principle of cells.

2

How I came to accept Jesus

I never believed in Jesus when I lived in Korea. In fact, I used to
criticize the people who talked about Jesus because it sounded
ridiculous to me. Although Ewha Woman's University was a mission
school, I refused to bow my head or close my eyes during the prayer
time in chapel. Since chapel was mandatory, I just sat there to receive
credit.

When I visited my home in Jinju during the breaks, my sister would
tell me that if I didn't believe in Jesus, I would end up going to Hell.
I was so offended that I threw back some very hurtful words to her.

My sister at the time was studying Mathematics in Kyung-Nam
University; and since her freshman year, she had been involved in

Cru (Campus Crusade for Christ) and had thus accepted Jesus as her personal Savior. Her faith in the Lord was growing during that time, so whenever I visited home every six months, she seized the opportunity to share about the Gospel to me. She kept on saying I could only go to Heaven if I believed in Jesus to the extent that I got very frustrated and annoyed at her.

However, the reason why I couldn't believe in Jesus at that time was largely because I, being a rational medical student, could not accept the fact that Jesus was born from a virgin. It just did not make any sense to me; so even before I heard about the Gospel, I had already rejected Jesus and Christianity.

However, on the bus ride back to Seoul, I remember thinking, "Who is this Jesus? Who is this One that my sister implores me with tears to believe in?" I had no way of knowing, but there were times when I thought that if God was real, He probably would punish me for rejecting Him.

Then I came to the United States after being admitted to Brown University, a private Ivy League research university located in the small city of Providence, Rhode Island. The reason I decided to come to Brown University was because the school had offered to grant me a scholarship of $30,000 a year. When I first arrived at the school dormitory, I was given a roasted steak with no seasonings, with bread and butter on the side. I could not eat it. I was too accustomed to

Korean food that I couldn't eat the dorm foods, which were mainly western dishes. I couldn't even go to the dorm cafeteria because I couldn't stand the smell of the food.

I ended up losing about 8 lbs. in 2 weeks (I went down from 100 lbs. to 92 lbs.). Strangely, there were no Korean markets or even Korean restaurants in the city. The only food that I could eat was Japanese ramen, which was a dollar for four packages. So every day, three meals a day, I had Japanese ramen topped with Tabasco hot sauce. Two weeks then passed without any access to Korean food. Then one Sunday morning, a graduate student who was studying microbiology at the same school knocked on my room in the dorm. She came to tell me about a Korean church in the city and added that they provide a buffet of Korean foods after the service every week and that you could meet new Korean friends and talk in Korean as much as you want. She then asked me if I was interested in joining her to church. Church was definitely not my thing, but my heart was stirred up by the fact that there was going to be Korean food. So I willingly tagged along with her to church.

My biggest purpose for going to church on Sundays was to eat Korean food. Listening to the pastor's sermon for about an hour for a decent Korean meal seemed like a good deal after all. But to tell the truth, a part of me wanted to go to church out of curiosity because of my sister.

I ended up going to church for about 8 consecutive weeks. Church was a great stress-buster for me because I could eat Korean food and speak in Korean as much as I wanted to. Then on the eighth Sunday, while I was listening to the pastor's sermon at church, his words suddenly pierced through my heart. Then God became real in my life, and tears started streaming down my cheeks endlessly. Regrets about having rejected Him for all these years flooded in at the same time.

Nobody had taught me before, but it just hit me at that moment that the greatest sin a person could ever commit is to deny that God really exists. As I came to believe that there is a God, the whole creation story became real to me as well. Although I had never read a single page of the Bible before, I suddenly had faith that everything in the Bible must be true.

Then I thought, *If God had really created the heavens and the earth and even mankind, then God must also have sent Jesus to earth through a virgin.* Hallelujah! I was able to accept all of these by faith. God miraculously intervened in my life that day and changed my whole perception around. It was truly a miracle.

As soon as I came back to the dorm that Sunday, the first thing I did was to call my sister in Korea. I had come to believe in Jesus exactly 10 weeks after my arrival in the United States. Hallelujah! I told my sister in tears, "Sister, I now believe in Jesus."

My sister did not know what to say. She cried for joy at the news and praised God for working in me. For the first time in my life, I was more grateful for my sister than my biological parents because she had been praying for me for six years (This may sadden my mother if she hears this, though). It doesn't matter because I strongly believe that it was my sister's fervent intercession that led me to put my faith in Jesus.

So I finally accepted Jesus as my personal Savior, with tears. Strangely, since the day I accepted Jesus as my Lord, I became a crybaby. I cried whenever I heard about God. My church people would often ask me if I was okay. It was hard to explain, but I wept and wept. I couldn't stop my tears from falling down. I was crying out of a repentant heart for having denied God's existence all these times, and I was also crying out of gratitude towards God for saving a wretch like me. I remember crying like that every day for about three years.

3

My superficial religious life for 6 years

Unfortunately, regardless of how I came to believe in God and how sincerely I had accepted Jesus to be my Christ and Savior, my old self and the purpose of my life did not change overnight. The only thing that changed in my life was a slight adjustment to my goal. Although my paradigm had shifted from being an atheist to a believer in God, my dream of becoming a notable scientist in the world did not change. I knew I had to strive to live for the glory of God, but I didn't exactly know what that meant in my life. So I just decided I would give glory to God when I become a famous scientist. I believed that showing the nonbelievers that there are well respected and notable Christian scientists would glorify God's name. That was the depth of my faith.

Regardless of being saved by God's grace, I wasn't living my life as a child of God, for He was not yet the purpose of my life. I did believe in God, but my faith was very shallow and I was in pursuit of my own success and fame. This continued for about six years.

Nevertheless, I never failed to give my tithe offerings and I never missed church on Sundays. I didn't completely understand why these two were so important, but I followed them anyway because that is what my sister had advised me to do. She actually told me that I would die if I didn't follow them. I didn't have a choice but to listen to her words because she had played a crucial part in leading me to Christ. Two of these basic practices brought many blessings to my life, although I did them without knowing what to expect. I learned that God really finds delight in these two things.

However, God did not leave me to continue my life this way. A major breakthrough happened in my faith journey when I heard the voice of God one day.

4

The audible voice of the Lord

I was at a three-day church retreat in Big Bear. It happened while I was listening to a church brother's testimony. In three months, he was about to receive his doctoral degree in Economics in UCLA. Earlier, I had heard from other people that he was planning to leave for missions after his graduation; and I remember responding, "He must be crazy! How can he leave for missions after getting his Ph.D.? What a waste!"

This very brother was sharing his testimony during the retreat. My eyes widened. *Isn't he the guy who said he would leave for missions after his Ph.D.?* I pricked up my ears not to miss a word.

He had been voluntarily serving at a Bible Study group that consisted of about 140 college and graduate students. His job was to organize the chairs for the bible study, by unfolding them before the meeting and folding them back to place afterwards. I was actually in that Bible study too. He was sharing that he had been in charge of organizing the chairs with one other person; but since that person got sick, he had to do it all by himself. He said he became a bit frustrated because it then took him an hour to get everything done, when it normally took 30 minutes. He also got upset thinking about the whole situation of him doing such a trivial task when he was going to be getting his Ph.D. in just three months.

There were about 100 people listening to this brother's testimony at the time, and the audiences were all sitting in round tables in groups of six. I too was sitting in a round table and listening to him intently when the Holy Spirit suddenly convicted me and touched me in an irresistible way. A thought came into my mind. *You know, you don't necessarily need to have a Ph.D. to serve God!* But the thought of how much I have labored all these years to come this far and even to the United States surged in my head, and I began to cry because I felt like I has done all of this in vain.

I was 35 years old at that time. I was convicted that I wasn't living the life I was called to live, so I bitterly wept and wept.

I was not sure *for what* I had been living all this time. Oh, how I wished I could go somewhere and just cry my heart out. I couldn't stay still in the chair so I stood up and went to my room, locked the door and began bawling. I had never cried so loudly in my life before.

For what have I come this far? For what? Not once in my life have I ever got to attend the school festival. Not once have I ever had a real vacation. Not once have I ever enjoyed a hobby of my own. All these years, I have lived only for studies and academic degrees, to become the best and to receive recognition! And here I am crying like an animal.

It was when all these mixed emotions and thoughts rushed inside of me that I heard the voice of God. (I am not exactly sure whether the voice was heard within my heart or outside, but His voice was very clear and distinct).

"Sang-ah, you will come to Heaven when you die."

I replied, "Yes, God, I know. I know I will come to Heaven because I believe that Jesus is my Savior." Then God began to speak to me in English.

"If you come to Heaven, I will ask you only one question."

So I asked, "What? What will you ask me?"

And He clearly said in English, "I will ask 'What did you do for me in this life?'" When I heard this, I had to quickly think of something to say because this was a divine moment of connection between the Creator and His creation. Nobody can refuse before the power of the Almighty One.

"Lord, there's nothing else that I am good at besides studying. The only think I know how to do besides studying is driving, but you know that I have a poor sense of direction. I will probably live for 30-40 more years; so if I really work hard in the lab, I think I will be able to write about 100 research papers."

This was the answer I had come up with in my head and was about to say it to God when, all of a sudden, I saw a vision of myself holding 100 research papers before God. I was certainly standing before His holy presence, although I could only see the lower end of His white gown. I was holding my 100 research papers with two hands and slowly stood up. Then when I was about to say, "God, I have been writing all these papers for you," all the papers I have put so much time and effort in suddenly looked pointless before my eyes.

It was a shocking moment of truth when I realized that even though I had worked my whole life to write all those papers, they were nothing more than a piece of tissue paper before God's eyes. Since God is the Author of this whole universe, every research paper that gets published is nothing more than a small disclosure about the mechanism of God's divine creation. Thus, research papers don't hold much value in His eyes.

The moment I realized how worthless these research papers are and that this wasn't what God was really interested in, I began to weep even more bitterly. While I was crying, God placed in my mind something I had never thought of before. He made me realize that if I had 40 more years to live from now (unless I die from a sudden disease or a car accident), that wouldn't be short after all. And if I were to use those years for God, it would actually be quite a long time.

It suddenly dawned on me that instead of spending the remaining forty years of my life in the lab writing research papers, if I choose to spend my time and strength saving lost souls in needy places (at that moment, I saw a vision of a basket that is used to carry souls), then I would at least be able to save 30,000 to 40,000 souls and bring the basket of souls to Heaven.

Then again, I saw a vision of myself before the presence of God. On my left hand, I was holding 100 research papers; while on my right, I was holding a basket full of souls. That was it. It became clear to me at that very moment. What God desired of me is not to live my life writing papers, but saving souls.

After I received this revelation, I began to cry again. I cried so hard. This was a wake-up call from God. I knew that God was transforming me at that moment to become His vessel. Thus, from then on, I began to deeply ponder about the things I ought to give Him and the things I ought to discard in my life if I was really serious about living my life for God.

When my father passed away, he had left me some of his inheritance. With this in mind, it became clear to me that I should give this to the Lord and use it to save the lost souls. I was also deeply convicted that I needed to get rid of my worldly desire for fame and honor.

I began to weep again because it was so painful to think of all the time and energy I had poured out all these years for nothing. I couldn't understand why God had not called me earlier, at least when I was in my 20s before all the stressful years of studying began. I was so upset for all the time that had been lost.

After two hours had passed, all the crying and wailing stopped. I opened the door of my room, but strangely, the air outside seemed somewhat different. Everything looked and felt different. All the trees on the mountains were even singing songs for me. Most of all, I had a new heart for lost souls. It occurred to me that everybody, regardless of their race and ethnicity, is very precious in God's eyes and that nobody is superior to the other.

Once I had stopped crying, I had been transformed to a whole new person. I felt like I was born again. No, I *was* born again, to a whole new creation. I was no longer the old self who used to pursue fame and honor. My life completely turned around as my life's purpose now pointed to God alone. I became a new person after I understood the life God desired me to pursue. In the past, I had done research to gain credit and recognition; but after the retreat, research became no more than a means to make ends meet in order for me to live for God. Hallelujah!

Philippians 3:4-9

"Though I myself have reason for confidence in the flesh also. If anyone else thinks he has reason for confidence in the flesh, I have more: circumcised on the eighth day, of the people of Israel, of the tribe of Benjamin, a Hebrew of Hebrews; as to the law, a Pharisee; as to zeal, a persecutor of the church; as to righteousness under the law, blameless. But whatever gain I had, I counted as loss for the sake of Christ. Indeed, I count everything as loss because of the surpassing worth of knowing Christ Jesus my Lord. For his sake I have suffered the loss of all things and count them as rubbish, in order that I may gain Christ and be found in him, not having a righteousness of my own that comes from the law, but that which comes through faith in Christ, the righteousness from God that depends on faith."

5

Becoming a fisher of souls

Ever since I was born again, I spent most of my time sharing the Gospel to the Korean students in UCLA. I even found myself not being able to focus on reading research papers because they didn't mean much to me anymore. While I used to pile up about a hundred research materials on my table and skim through them all, now I could not even go over a single page. I felt no motivation because it was no longer my passion.

God had evidently changed the purpose and passion of my life completely about.

As a result, some major changes surfaced in my life. *I* was no longer the center of my life; I have begun to live only for God and others. Hallelujah!

Most of my time and energy was now spent in evangelizing to Korean students in UCLA, instead of in the lab and writing research theses. I was so passionate to share the Gospel to the Korean students during lunch hours; and once I came home from school, I drove to Korea Town and to do open-air evangelism for hours. This continued every day for about two months.

6

Fired from work

One day, my adviser called me in and told me to quit my postdoctoral fellowship. He/she said I was obviously not interested in my lab work anymore, since I have been obsessed with evangelizing and was even seen praying on my knees in the lab on Saturdays. My adviser had made the decision that I was no longer needed in the lab.

So I replied, "You should believe in Jesus too." The adviser's face suddenly turned red. He/she became furious.

I knew this day would come but didn't expect it to come this fast. Just like that, I got fired from UCLA.

However, I urgently needed a job to get by, so I immediately applied for a postdoctoral program in USC. Thankfully, the school responded right away and offered me the opportunity to start working in September, which was two months away. So during the two months, I packed up all my belongings and put them in the storage place. I then decided to go to the prayer mountain because I was completely broke.

A month earlier I had given my savings as a mission offering for Africa. (It was actually the savings I had kept for my wedding, but God had spoken to me very clearly in Big Bear that the money in my savings account was not mine. So after wrestling for about a year, I finally decided to use it for God).

I barely had enough money to pay for my basic expenses when I got fired because based on what I was earning from UCLA, I was paying all my bills and was even taking a class in the seminary. I could only take one because a single class was worth $1,000.

But strangely enough, two days before I was fired, I heard the voice of God while I was praying. He said that He would use all that I have, including all my fingers. I laughed and asked Him, "What do you mean you will even use my fingers when I am using them to conducts tests in the lab?"

I got fired two days later.

Even then, I still didn't fully understand what God had meant when He had spoken to me earlier. I didn't understand what He meant when he said to seek first the Kingdom of God and His righteousness, and all these things shall be added unto you. I actually didn't even know such passage existed in the Bible.

So in hopes of finding a job to make a living, I applied right away to another postdoctoral program at USC. However, my heart was not at peace.

My heart was burning so passionately for God and for the Gospel that I didn't know what to do. I felt like there was dynamite for the lost souls inside of me that was about to explode. I also felt like I would end up getting fired again in USC for evangelizing rather than working in the lab. So I began praying and fasting before God. I sought for His direction, for I was completely lost. I wanted confirmation from God, whether I should live for Him while working in the lab and writing research papers, or whether I should just trust in Him with my financial needs and choose the path to full-time ministry.

I was going through an identity crisis regarding who I was and how I should live from now on. I thought that God would bless me for how hard I had worked to evangelize people. But in contrast to what I have expected, I ended up becoming jobless and penniless. So I had no choice but to stay in the prayer mountain since I had nowhere else to go.

I had become a homeless person in one day.

I couldn't dare to pursue a career in academia anymore even if I had a doctoral degree because I knew that wasn't the path for me. God had taken away my passion for science, so I had basically become a useless person. It was only natural that I started going through an identity crisis about who I was. I was also overshadowed with fear that I would no longer be able to work in the secular world.

USC was waiting to work with me after two months, but I didn't feel right about it. I had a feeling I would get kicked out again within six months because of my burning passion for the Gospel. So I began fasting. I was desperate to know His will.

On my sixth day of fasting, a deaconess approached me and asked, "Are you all right? Is there something that is bothering you?" So I told her the reason why I was fasting and that I was seeking for God's direction. She then offered me a piece of advice. She was truly a Godsend. She told me that if I will choose the path of God, God would take care of the rest. That was the voice of God that I had been yearning for.

I determined that I had been called to give up secular jobs and commit my life fully to God's work. So I ended my fast and made a final decision not to go to USC. I wrote a letter to USC and said that I had to reject their offer because I was no longer going to take the path of a scientist; that I would seek to find the Truth in God and the Bible. I also wrote that before I knew God, I had falsely believed that Science would lead me to the Truth. But now I had discovered that I was wrong, so I was changing my course. I also said I was sorry.

Since that day, my life has had nothing to do with science. Just as God had told me 2 days before I got fired from UCLA, I gave all of myself to God for Him to use me. Hallelujah!

I felt so free, and an immense peace covered me. Choosing God over the world brought so much freedom in my spirit, even if I was left with nothing from a worldly perspective.

7

God's provision for my seminary tuition

I now needed to seek support to fill my seminary tuition, so I began to pray. Since I had no income, I had to find supporters to be able to attend seminary. I cried out to God every day and night at church and was determined to pray until God would send me supporters, be it six months or one year. But raising support was harder than I thought it would be.

I then wrote a long letter to the president of a record company, who had told me some time ago that he would support me if I go out for missions. I explained to him my whole story and that I needed support to attend seminary. He wrote me back but said he won't be able to support me because the business was going through a rough patch.

I then listed the names of several people and began to pray. As I prayed for each one of them, I asked the Lord whether he or she was the one to be my supporter. But the Lord said 'no' to all of them.

"Then what should I do?" I asked.

And the Lord said, "Do not be anxious. Your tuition for seminary has already been provided for in the world."

But I retorted, "Anybody can say that! Of course I know that everything is provided in the world, but don't I at least have to know through whom it will be provided?"

The next day, I stopped by the seminary because I had to change my visa to a student visa; my working visa was no longer valid from the day I was fired. The counselor at the office happened to be a Korean. I explained to her the whole story because I thought I needed to give her a reasonable reason for changing my visa status. I was very fortunate because everything worked out very smoothly. Then just as I was about to leave the office, the counselor stopped me and said, "Wait." She asked me, "Then how are you going to pay for your tuition?"

Still holding onto the doorknob, I turned around and said, "Pray for me. That's exactly why I am in the prayer mountain right now. No matter how long it may take, I am going to pray that I will meet supporters to help provide my tuitions. Pray for me."

Right after I said these words, I pulled the doorknob and was about to go out when the counselor spoke again, "Wait. Wait. Come back in." So I went back in the office and sat down.

The counselor suddenly opened the drawer next to her table and took out a thick packet of papers. Handing me those papers, she said, "Then write your financial situation in full details here and try applying for this scholarship. This scholarship will cover from 50% up to 80% of the tuition for seminary students."

The moment I received this scholarship application form, I knew instantly that it was from God. It became clear why God had said that my tuition was already provided. I was overjoyed. I was filled with so much joy for God's answer to my prayer that I took the scholarship application form to the altar and praised God the whole night. Hallelujah!

After spending a few days filling the application form, I finally submitted it to school. I was 100% certain that this was God's answer to my prayer. But then I began to hear from the senior seminary students that there had never been a Korean recipient of that scholarship up to that point. They told me that the scholarship was usually given to those who have been in the mission field for over five years, or to those who were from a third world country, such as in Africa, and were planning to become a pastor and return to their home country to do full-time ministry. So they explained how unlikely it was for me to be selected. Nevertheless, I had faith deep inside that I would receive that scholarship.

After several months had passed, I was finally informed that I had been selected as the recipient of the scholarship and that it will cover half of my tuition fee. Later on, I received even more – 80% of funding.

I cried because I was so humbled. God had really provided all my needs because I chose to walk in His way.

I needed 30,000 dollars in order to graduate from the seminary, and God has indeed provided almost everything. I would never have been able to pay that amount on my own even if I were working.

Even when I was jobless, and when all I did was to read the Bible, pray, and evangelize, He knew my needs and provided them just in time. Although I had to stay at the prayer mountain since I had no house, God took care of the rest.

Luke 12:29-31

"And do not seek what you are to eat and what you are to drink, nor be worried. For all the nations of the world seek after these things, and your Father knows that you need them. Instead, seek his kingdom, and these things will be added to you."

8

God's calling

I never planned on studying theology because I was so sick of studying in general. I knew that the Lord had called me into full time ministry, but I assumed that He was going to lead me to become a pastor's wife.

However, after I heard God's voice in Big Bear, while I was in a Bible Study that was led by an elder, a passage from the Bible hit me very hard. It was from **1 Thessalonians 5:24, "He who calls you is faithful; he will surely do it."**

My heart started pounding so loud that I could even hear the sound of my heartbeat for the first time in my life. The word of God spoke to me so powerfully that I could not remember what the elder had taught that day. As I came home that night, I knelt down in my living room and asked God why this passage would not leave my mind. Then the Lord said to carry this word and go up to the prayer mountain.

So I immediately packed up my things and went to the prayer mountain and fasted for 3 days. I cried out to God inside the prayer closet. I later found myself speaking out all these unfamiliar prophetic words. Words that I had not even thought of, such as "I have called you for my glory," came out of my mouth.

On the second day of fasting, I was so weak so I went for a drive near the prayer mountain to a place called Lake Street. After I made a turn around a long curve, there before me was a linear road with trees aligned in both sides. That day, the sky was very blue and beautiful, covered with clear clouds.

All of a sudden, the glory of God came down heavily upon that place right where I was. I could not drive any further; I had to pull over at the side. His glory felt like an invisible wall that could not be surpassed. Fear and reverence covered my whole being, but I knew instantly it was the glory of God that was surrounding me.

Before His glory was taken away, I desperately wanted to receive a word from God. So I humbly said, "God, please speak to me." I asked this because I was well aware that His glory would disappear soon, but His word will remain in my heart for life.

Then the voice of God came.

"Sang-ah, when I created the world, was there a time when I needed to repeat what I had already said?"

In other words, He was asking if there was a time when He had said something but nothing happened that He had to say it over again. So I replied, "No. You only had to speak once and things were created."

And He continued, "In the same way, I do not have to repeat what I have told you before. What has come out of my mouth will not be reversed."

Hallelujah!

At that moment, I remembered what the Lord had said to me before.

He had told me that He would use me.

And God was telling me that day He was not going to change His mind.

That is how I interpreted His words but as time passed by, I gained a new insight into what He also meant that day. It was that none of His words in the Bible will ever be revoked. Hallelujah!

Just like that, my brief conversation with God ended and His glory that had filled the place lifted completely. I then drove to the far end of the road and returned to the very place where His glory had manifested, hoping it would happen again. But it did not.

On the third day of fasting, I went to the worship sanctuary to attend the morning service for the last time before I headed home. The pastor was reading the Scripture from Isaiah 55 and as she/he was reading through the chapter, a specific verse from the passage struck me again.

Isaiah 55:12

"For you shall go out in joy and be led forth in peace; the mountains and the hills before you shall break forth into singing, and all the trees of the field shall clap their hands."

The clause "you shall go out in joy and be led forth in peace" specifically spoke to my heart very powerfully. The reason why I had come to the prayer mountain and fasted in the first place was because of His word "He who calls you is faithful; he will surely do it." It was just amazing how it connected so well with the word He was giving me right before I headed back home: "You shall go out in joy and be led forth in peace."

I may not know what God looks like, but having received these two promises from God, I could not deny that God has indeed manifested Himself to me. My heart started pounding again. *Hallelujah. I praise You, Lord. This was why You led me to the prayer mountain.*

Another startling thing was that Isaiah 55:11, the previous verse in the same passage, was almost identical to what God had said to me at Lake Street.

Isaiah 55:11

"So shall my word be that goes out from my mouth; it shall n return to me empty, but it shall accomplish that which I purpos and shall succeed in the thing for which I sent it."

The pastor had been reading from Isaiah 55:8-12 during the morning service, and I was once again awed by each of the verses. I strongly believe that God purposefully used this pastor and the elder to speak to me and encourage me in a very timely manner. So I left the prayer mountain with a joyful spirit.

Eventually, it took me about seven years to graduate from the seminary. I was ordained shortly after because God had called me to plant a church. This is how the Lord's Love Christian Church in Glendale, which is located about 20 minutes away from Korea Town in Los Angeles, began. Currently, I am also leading a small church in Korea Town. I am willing to stay until God tells me to do otherwise, so I am constantly on call for His mission.

Because God had spoken to me to go out in joy and be led forth in peace, I am doing His work with joy and passion for missions to this day.

Isaiah 55:8-13

"For my thoughts are not your thoughts, neither are your ways my ways, declares the LORD.

or as the heavens are higher than the earth, so are my ways higher than your ways and my thoughts than your thoughts.

For as the rain and the snow come down from heaven and do not return there but water the earth, making it bring forth and sprout, giving seed to the sower and bread to the eater, so shall my word be that goes out from my mouth; it shall not return to me empty, but it shall accomplish that which I purpose, and shall succeed in the thing for which I sent it.

For you shall go out in joy and be led forth in peace; the mountains and the hills before you shall break forth into singing, and all the trees of the field shall clap their hands.

Instead of the thorn shall come up the cypress; instead of the brier shall come up the myrtle; and it shall make a name for the LORD, an everlasting sign that shall not be cut off."

SPONSORSHIP PAGE

Matthew 6:31-33

"Therefore do not be anxious, saying, 'What shall we eat?' or 'What shall we drink?' or 'What shall we wear?' For the Gentiles seek after all these things, and your heavenly Father knows that you need them all. But seek first the kingdom of God and his righteousness, and all these things will be added to you."

Your financial support to this ministry is greatly appreciated! It will be used to publish this book in both Korean and English, with the hope of being used as a mighty tool for the Gospel to reach around the world.

Your support will also be used to hold testimonial revival services to reach out to lost souls and lead them to Jesus Christ.

Please support our ministry to save more lives by your generosity according to the leading of the Holy Spirit.

■ All funds will only be used for the purpose of saving souls and expanding the Kingdom of God.

You can also donate in her hompage, www.pastorsarah.org. by Clicking 'tithing and offering'

Account information:

Paypal account:

lordslovechristianchurch@yahoo.com

or

sarahseoh@ymail.com